Jefferson Davis

Ghosts, *Critters*
&
Sacred Places
Of
Washington
and
Oregon II

By Jefferson Davis

First Printing 2000

Printed by Central Plains Book Manufacturing, Winfield, Kansas

Library of Congress Number: 00-104102
Davis, Jefferson Dale
    Ghosts, Critters & Sacred Places of Washington and Oregon II
            1. Native Americans
            2. Spirituality, Parapsychology and Folklore
            3. Oregon and Washington History
            4. Includes Index
ISBN: 1-893186-02-4

Acknowledgments

Thanks to the friendly native guides who took me to many different locations in the Pacific Northwest when I wrote this book. They are Kaycee White, Tony Popp, Karan, Karin and Karen. Thanks to Spokane's newspaper reporter and guitar player, Doug Clark. Thank you Red Elk for your story and insight.

On the technical end, thank you Theresa for proofing the draft of this book. Thanks Zen-website-guru John Goodman for your tireless upgrades of my homepage. Thank you Su at Stone Crow Graphics for the great cover art.

Preface

Welcome to my third book, *Ghosts, Critters and Sacred Places of Washington and Oregon II.* From now on, I will use this title and add a number to denote the latest book of new stories. I intended to use a new title for each book, but changed my mind for a two reasons. Firstly, some people have seen my first book, *Ghosts and Strange Critters of Washington and Oregon*, and thought my second book, *Ghosts, Critters and Sacred Places of Washington and Oregon* were the same book. This is not true, but people had trouble telling the difference. Secondly, I had a hard time thinking up a better title.

For those of you who have my other books (Bless You!), this one follows the same format as my others. It contains all new stories from haunted and sacred places in the Northwest. There are Indian sites, time slips, firewalking and many haunted public places. I have included an in-depth discussion of ghost photography and more critters. There are a few familiar sites from my other books, where the ghosts continued their hauntings and I updated their story.

There are some differences from my earlier books. I was not able to gather enough stories from Eastern Oregon to make a whole section. I'll have more stories in the next book. Another change came from reader comments. During a book signing tour last October; some readers asked me to include more pictures and artwork in this book, which I did.

Many of these haunts are open to the public, except where I have a warning about no visitors. Wherever you go, remember that you're a guest, so please respect the rights of the property owners. If you have stories that you want to tell, please write me at **PO Box 4803, Vancouver, WA 98662.** You can visit my home page at **www.pacifier.com/~jpaul** or contact me at **jddavis@rocketmail.com**.-Jeff Davis

Jefferson Davis

Table of Contents

5

Introduction

A recent Gallup Poll found that 30% of the people in America believe in ghosts. This does not include the people who are willing to at least discuss the possibility of their existence. Other people do not believe in ghosts and that is the end of the discussion. Other people have different theories as to what causes the phenomena we commonly refer to as ghosts. Still other people are curious and unconvinced and wait for more information. For these people I will try and give a brief background on the paranormal phenomena of ghosts and hauntings.

There is a lot of perfectly natural phenomenon that has been mistaken for ghosts and hauntings. These can be something as simple as a high tide or underground stream causing houses to shake or shudder. The shadow of a branch waving in a breeze, when seen through a window can cause shadows to creep inside a house when the branch is backlit by a streetlight. Another branch scraping against of a house or rodents living in the crawlspaces can create some scary sounds in daylight as well as at night. These are fairly easy to detect if you keep your head and investigate. There are other natural phenomenon that are harder to detect.

It has been proven that subtle natural energies can mimic the effects we expect from ghosts. Some forms of sound energy can affect the human senses and cause people to feel anxiety, fear and even see hallucinations. The human brain works by a complex series of bio-electrical impulses and energy. What would happen if our brains and bodies were subjected to large amounts of energies that we do not ordinarily experience?

Human senses are limited in many ways. There may be a sixth sense, which allows us to perceive energies that are not perceptible to the normal senses of sight, hearing, smell, taste and touch. The field of psychic investigation is part and parcel of parapsychology. In addition to human ghost senses, people have been trying to invent mechanical devices to detect the paranormal for over a century. Some people believe that a common household device, the camera can detect the presence of paranormal events because its senses, namely specialty films like infrared film, can detect energy outside of the range of human vision. For a discussion of how a camera and infrared film works and hints on how not to be fooled by natural phenomena, see *Thoughts on Ghosts and Ghost Hunting*, in this book.

The mass and composition of mountains or geologic deposits can affect both gravity and the earth's magnetic field. This is usually very subtle, but has been documented in a variety of places from the Himalayas to Neolithic quarries in Brittany, where stone was cut to build ancient standing stones. How does this affect human beings? Some people claim that they are sensitive to the sub-sonic vibrations of developing earthquakes. Other people have made similar claims about being affected by magnetic fields. It is a fact that in hydroelectric plants, the magnetic flux is so strong that it can "pull" on the iron in human blood. What might sensitive people find?

There are several cases in this book where people have experienced something Parapsychologists have come to call time slip phenomenon. This is not necessarily a haunting, since there is not a ghost. It is more like a person has been transported or can see backward in time. They perceive a building or place that looks like it did sometime in the past. Like the phantom picture an employee at the Edgefield poorhouse in the Gorge saw. This disappeared when she tried to show it to another employee. Sometimes the person experiencing a time slip will see people going about their business, who may or may not perceive them. Sometimes they interact with the other people, like the two hikers on the Indian Beach trail on the Oregon coast. As an extreme example, there is the couple who ate at a phantom restaurant in Spokane. What natural energy can cause this?

After Carl Sagan's *Cosmos* program and years of all those *Star Trek* shows, most people in America know that space is curved. According to Einstein and Sagan, if you go in any one direction long enough, you will eventually come back to your starting point. Space is curved, but that does not mean time is curved the same way. When you come back to your starting point, time has passed. If time is curved, does it follow the same path round as space? Some believe that time is part of the fourth dimension. Because we live in a three dimensional world, we can perceive time and we are affected by its passage. Yet our senses cannot completely perceive, see, hear, touch, taste or smell all aspects of time.

It makes sense that if space and time exist on separate planes of existence, they are not completely tied to each other. There are already scientific discoveries or theories about anomalies in space, like black holes, dark matter and anti-matter. What if there is anti-time? Or places where we can perceive other times? There is a theory that time is fluid, like a river. Rivers do not flow at a constant rate. What if time does the same thing? That might explain how sometimes a minute or an hour seems to drag along or an hour can pass like a minute. Time changes its flow, but our bio-electric energy does not? After all, electricity flows at the speed of light, no slower, no faster. Right? Physicists theorize that space can be warped, why not time?

If you follow a model where time flows like a river, in addition to rapids and pools, there may be eddies and bends as well. What if time can loop back on itself, where in one place time flows close to another loop in the time continuum. Would it be possible to see from one point in time to another? Like standing on a river bank, looking across the river bend. Some people have abnormal bio-electric fields. Could they detect this loop?

There are certain places like the Oregon Vortex, where the magnetic field of the Earth is a little strange. See, *The mysteries of the Oregon Vortex,* in this book. The owners of the property maintain that both space and possibly time are warped there. This could be true in other places across the world. It could also explain the disappearances of thousands of people worldwide each year. Their loss might not be a case of running away. Some people may not be able to just see over time, but they can stepp back into it as well.

If that is too uncomfortable, there are the more conventional theories about ghosts. The simplest definition of a ghost is that a ghost is the spiritual remains of a deceased person, which remains on earth instead of passing on to a different plain of existence. Not a simple definition, is it? Another definition is that a ghost is basically a soul without a body. It can manifest itself in many paranormal ways, such as being seen, heard, felt, touched or even smelled. A haunting should be defined as several paranormal events in a common setting.

Most hauntings are associated with buildings or places. In some cases, when the buildings are torn down, the haunting ceases. In other cases, the hauntings continue in the vacant lot or new structure, like the Spokane Civic Theater? The haunting may not be tied to a location.

It could be tied to a person or thing. Poltergeists are usually attached to children and follow them from place to place. Mythical curses follow people around. There are also examples of haunted houses being moved and the ghost moves with them. Some ghosts seem to be attached to certain objects, such as a camcorder which had belonged to the first husband of a woman from Grant's Passes, that stopped working during her wedding, when she remarried.

One of the questions about ghosts is, why do we see them mostly at night? Aren't they there during the day? Maybe they are and we just don't perceive them as such. If ghosts are solid looking, we may think that they are living beings. We may just look at them differently if we see them in places they should not be, like a dark, empty building. Then again, we may still see ghosts in unexpected places and times and we see them as living beings, because they are still carrying on business as usual. Like the security guard who haunts the campus at Ashland's Southern Oregon University; who opens office doors for faculty members.

A very common type of ghost that usually does not lead to a haunting is the apparition of a living person. A person wakes up in the middle of the night to see a spouse or loved one, standing beside their bed. The figure may say goodbye or just look at them and then disappear. Some days or weeks later the sleeper finds out that their loved one has died. In other cases, the person whose apparition was seen is still alive, though stressed. After this single occurrence the apparition usually does not appear again.

The most common type of ghost seems to be a kind of snapshot in time. Frequently, violent or traumatic events seem to release an energy that imprints the action on a place or object. In this kind of haunting, the violent action repeats itself, like a videotape rewound and played over and over again. Sometimes it is not violent action. It can be the result of someone performing the same actions over and over again, like a night watchman making his rounds. This somehow imprint itself on a place after the person is dead or gone.

These hauntings can be seen, heard, felt or even smelled. Ghosts are frequently seen at the same time every night, or at certain seasons of the year. They are not doing anything remarkable, they are just going about their business, like a maid cleaning rooms or a night watchman making his rounds. The ghosts are not aware that their surroundings have changed. That is why some ghosts appear walking though solid walls, where there used to be a doorway. They may also walk above or below a modern floor. Their surroundings have changed but the ghosts have not. Parishioner at the old Nordic Church in Ridgefield, WA, once saw this, when they observed ghostly worshipers walking below the current church floor level.

The self-aware spirit is another kind of haunting. In this case, spirits continue to exist in places where they lived or worked, after their death. These spirits often stay on because they have business they want to finish. Sometimes they want to pass on information about their life, death or something more important than life itself (to them). They may be waiting for a friend, even after death. There are guardian spirits, who protect a secret or perhaps treasure. They may have suffered a tragedy in the past and want to warn others in similar circumstances. Some spirits stay on for no apparent reason, like poltergeists.

Poltergeists means "noisy ghost". They are quite evident because they cause things to move from place to place, make noise and generally upset the routine of their surroundings. Poltergeists are usually associated with children before or during puberty. Poltergeists usually fade as puberty ends. This kind of ghost seems to be faked most often by people.

Most ghosts seem to fade away over time. They are most energetic after whatever event creates them. As time goes by their manifestations become less frequent. At first some ghosts are seen, heard and felt. The visible apparition is both the most frightening and rarest kind of spirit phenomenon. They may be the rarest because it may take a lot of energy to project a visible image. As time goes by, ghosts generally fade away and may only be heard. They may act only on the anniversary of their creation. Even the noises fade over time, until nothing is left of the ghost.

Other ghosts seem able to recharge themselves. Cold spots, light bulbs dimming, drained batters and electronic machinery going haywire may be the result of spirits gathering energy from around them. These cold spots are sometimes accompanied by erratic magnetic fields. Some people have suggested that these cold spots are actually doorways between a spiritual dimension and our own.

Another theory is that all ghostly phenomena is created by the energies of living people. One part of this theory is that ghosts do exist and they gather the energy to manifest themselves from their environment. They convert heat from a room into energy, which causes drops in temperature. This can include the energy from living beings.

The study of ghosts is only a small part of parapsychology. Far more money and time is spent researching the powers of the human mind. Just as the mind can create psychosomatic illnesses in the body, it may be able to create a ghost as a symptom of its beliefs or fears. Researchers speculate that some people who have seen ghosts are psychic who have read the minds of people, and convinced themselves that the information came from supernatural sources.

Still other people have speculated that some forms of mediumship, like the Ouiji board and crystal gazing are forms of hypnosis. The person doing the "scrying" or receiving visions is not psychic or under the influence of a spirit. They are actually using their subconscious abilities to pick up cues from their own memories and audience in a self-induced trance. There was a case where people created their own ghost as an experiment.

In the early 1970s a group of paranormal investigators from Toronto, Canada, experimented with psychic energies and created a ghost. They felt that it might be possible to create the illusion of a persona in their own minds and see if paranormal phenomena or a haunting would result. After several weeks of concentrating on their ghost, they were successful. This has of course come under a skeptical view that disputes the reality of these experiments and other ghostly phenomenon.

A skeptic is a person who looks at paranormal phenomenon and tries to find a reasonable explanation of what happened. To do this, skeptics prefer to perform their own investigations and then suggest scientific explanations for what has happened. Devout believers in the spirit world find themselves at odds with the skeptics at times. From my experience, the average skeptic wants to believe in ghosts as much as the "True-Believer", they just need more convincing. Look at the time, money and effort skeptics, like the Amazing Randi, spend investigating psychic phenomenon.

Skeptics can find rational and correct explanations for some alleged hauntings. However, some skeptics can come up with some highly detailed, unlikely, even improbable chains of coincidence when they try to rationalize or explain the paranormal. Sometimes it would be more likely to be struck by lightning rather than see a ghost.

The English philosopher William of Ockham, who died in 1349, coined a phrase that I like to use when looking at paranormal phenomena. He said (and I quote), *"pluralites non est ponenda sine necessitate."* For those readers who do not speak Latin, this roughly means; when trying to solve a problem with several different explanations, the simplest answer is probably the correct one. It's also called Ockham's Razor.

While researching this book, I took a photograph in a haunted house, which shows effects that were not visible when I took the picture. Because of this, I wrote an in-depth explanation of ghost photography in my *Thoughts on Ghost Hunting* section. This includes an explanation of how photography works and natural phenomenon that is often mistaken for ghostly emanations. The other discussion in this section is a look at the ancient practice of firewalking, which is alive and well in the Pacific Northwest. Whether you are a skeptic or a believer, you may find this interesting.

Native American Spirits and Sacred Places

Crater Lake, Oregon

The mountains of the Pacific Northwest are sacred to Native Americans. The higher the peak, the more people who see it, the more sacred it is. It is also possible for an ex-peak to become more sacred than a high one. An example of this is Crater Lake, which was once a 12,000 foot high mountain. It is known posthumously as Mount Mazama. Mount Mazama would have been one of the three highest peaks in the Oregon Cascade Mountains before it exploded.

Nearly 7,700 years ago, a series of eruptions shook Mount Mazama. The eruptions continued off and on for a thousand years, until they climaxed around 6,600 years ago. At that time, a series of cataclysmic eruptions shook the mountain. Over twenty-five cubic miles of ash and lava were ejected from the volcano. The ash was so widespread, it formed layers several inches thick in the Washington Cascades. The ash is so distinct that when archaeologists find it, they use it as a time marker for the site.

During the eruption 6,600 years ago, all of the lava was ejected from the center of the volcanic cone, leaving an empty center. The outer shell of the cone collapsed, forming a crater several thousand feet deep. In time the crater cooled and gradually filled with rain water and snow melt. The current depth of the lake is 1,932 feet. Because of the source of the water, it has a peculiar shade of deep blue.

The lake was sacred to Native Americans who lived in the area. Their shamans forbid the common Indian people from climbing to the top of the crater to look inside. There is a small island on the edge of the lake, known as Wizard's Island. It is called that because the shamans used to either swim or paddle out to the island in the summer and perform magic rituals there. They and their fellow tribesmen kept this secret for many years.

The earliest Euro-American exploration of Oregon took place when Lewis and Clark traveled through the northwest in the early 1800s. In the decades that followed, there were many other explorers who traveled through the area. None of them found its secret. Crater Lake was not "discovered" by Euro-Americans until the 1850s. In 1853, John W. Hillman stumbled upon the crater while he was searching for the Lost Cabin Gold Mine. Up to that time, all of the explorers and surveyors who hired native guides must have been carefully "guided" around the four mile by five mile wide crater by their smiling Indian guides.

Wizard Island is a recent feature of the lake. It is a cider cone that gradually poked its head out of the lake around 900 years ago. Did the shamans watch in awe, as the lake waters boiled and an island rose up from what they thought was a bottomless lake? Does the reverence Native people held for Crater Lake date to the fiery appearance of Wizard Island nearly a thousand years ago? Or does it date to the actual origin of the lake?

At the end of the last Ice Age, the area around Missoula Montana was a giant inland ocean. West of Missoula, the water was held back by a dam of ice and debris left behind by the retreating glaciers. The dam burst, reformed and burst again several times, sending giant floods west, through the Columbia River Gorge. The floods deposited everything from boulders the size of houses to very fine silts and clays. Native Americans on the Colville Indian Reservation told a story to an anthropologist that describes this phenomenon in detail. It also mentions a volcanic eruption that rained several inches of ash as far away as Missoula, Montana. Were there people in the Cascades 6,600 years ago who watched and survived the creation of Crater Lake?

Goose Lake, to kneel in prayer? (Gifford Pinchot National Forest)

I feel safe in mentioning this particular site at Goose Lake; even though it is still possible to visit that site. This is because it is impossible or rather unlikely that someone will deface or destroy this religious monument.

Visitors to the Gifford Pinchot National Forest's Trout Lake Ranger station are treated to a unique interpretive display. Mounted on the wall is a large plaster cast of a set of distinct handprints and footprints. This cast was made from an actual imprint in the solid rock that forms the floor of Goose Lake, several miles north of Trout Lake. The actual imprints are now safely hidden under the waters of the lake, but their origin is still under debate.

Some people believe that they were formed several thousand years ago, when the site of the lake was a large lava flow. According to Native American stories, a beautiful woman was being pursued by an evil brave. He chased her up to the top of Lemei Peak. From the top of the rock, she could see that the peak overlooked a lava flow. Faced with the threat of the man, or death from the lava, she chose death by jumping off the peak. She landed on the lava flow, feet first and then fell forward, burying her hands in the soft liquid rock. She died, and her ghost is supposed to appear on the shore of Goose Lake, combing her long hair.

She may have even survived this ordeal (see the article on Firewalking in the section on ghost hunting in this book). In memory of this event, people have returned for centuries afterward, perhaps believing the imprints to have been made by supernatural events. There is another theory to explain the mysterious hand and footprints.

Goose Lake is a place where native peoples may have waited for the sunrise of the summer solstice, the longest day of the year. Many Native American peoples like the Maya, Aztec, Inca and Anasazi actively studied astronomy. Fewer people realize that many Pacific Northwest Natives studied the relationship between the sun, moon and seasons. There are several locations in the northwest where native peoples celebrated the change of seasons. Of course, most of these places are located east of the Cascade Mountains, where you can count on having more sunny days.

Hundreds, or possibly thousands of years ago, someone may have knelt at the edge of Goose lake. They would have been there in the late summer, since Native Americans only gathered there in the summer and fall. They may have noticed how when they kneeled at this one spot that they could watch the sun rise over a high mountain peak to the east. There may have even been hollow spots in the lakebed that resembled handprints.

Over a period of hours, days or even years they returned to that spot and ground out a pair of handprints in the rock at the edge of the lake. In addition to the two handprints, they could have added a pair of holes below the handprints, to show people where to place their feet, so that they were facing the right direction. Shamans would have used this site for years, to help mark the change in seasons as fall turned to winter in the mountains.

Pioneers noted the hand and footprints in the late 1800s, and a newspaper article describing them appeared in 1890. Over the years, geologists and engineers examined the strange prints. Depending on their outlook, some of the experts proclaimed the prints werecarvings. Others claimed that they were real, and insisted that the handprints were real, and included fingerprints. Geologists speculated that the prints could be from 2,000 to 10,000 years old. In the 1930s, the outlet to Goose Lake, which was a sinkhole at the bottom of the lake, was dammed up. The water level rose, and the imprints disappeared under water. After that, many old-timers and curiosity seekers returned to Goose Lake in the hopes of seeing them. Except for a brief exposure during a drought in the 1960s, they were hidden under the lake.

It was not until the early 1990s, that a man named Larry King made a systematic search for them. He spent hundreds of hours floating on the surface of the lake on a raft, scanning the floor of the lake through a metal tube with a glass bottom. Eventually he located the handprints, under several feet of water. King and Forest Service personnel built a dam around the handprints and pumped the water out. They made a plaster cast of the prints, which now graces the wall of the Visitor's Center at Trout Lake. They removed the dam and the handprints were left to themselves, hidden underwater and a covering of mud and grass, but still there.

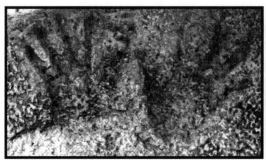

I examined the full-sized cast hanging on the wall of the Visitor's Center. I have seen examples of rock art over the years and this does not look like a carving to me. The footprints resemble soft soled moccasins, and the prints are over an inch deep into the rock. On the other hand, I did not see any great detail like fingerprints. Like many of the stories in this book, you will have to go there and decide for yourself.

Horsethief Lake State Park (located 17 miles east of White Salmon)

Horsethief Lake State Park is begins at the north bank of the Columbia River and extends north, into a small canyon in the hills of the Gorge. It received its name in the 1950s, when workers helping build the park thought that the narrow canyon would have been the perfect place for movie horsethieves to hide. The park includes 338 acres of land, with twelve campsites, thirty-five picnic sites, two boat launches and two miles of trails. Many people who visit the park are more concerned with day picnicking rather than the sacred places at the end of the trail leading into the canyon.

Inside this canyon there are several pieces of Native American art on the canyon wall. This artwork is a combination of petroglyphs (designs cut into rock) and pictographs (designs painted onto rock). The most impressive petroglyph is named Tsagigla'lal. One translation of this name is, *She who watches*. A longer translation of this name is, *She who watches and sees all who are coming and going up and down the river*. I make this distinction because they can mean two different things, and this affects the significance of this drawing and the dozens of other similar designs located in the canyon.

There are several legends surrounding this site. The most popular one is that in the past, women used to be chiefs of the people who lived along the river. One night Spilyai, the Great Spirit, came to the woman who was chief of a village near Horsethief Lake. Instead of living in the village, she lived in the hills overlooking her people, so that she could see what was happening inside and outside of the village to guard it better. Spilyai told her that the world was changing, and that women would no longer be chiefs. As a special favor to her, Spilyai turned her into a magical piece of rock art, so she could watch over her people. This role continued for centuries or thousands of years.

The Tsagigla'lal design may have also been used as a territorial marker. According to some stories, there was a matching pictograph on the south bank of the river, opposite the one at Horsethief Lake. There were also similar pictographs further down the Columbia River, marking the other end of this tribe's territory. Like many theories, there are  other interesting interpretations of the significance of Tsagigla'lal. One has to do with the way the meaning of symbols change over time.

Archaeologist James Keyser has studied rock art across the Pacific Northwest. He suggests that Tsagigla'lal was the primary symbol of a Native American death cult. With a shortened name of *She who watches*, the large eyes of Tsagigla'lal can be interpreted as being full of compassion. Tsagigla'lal style designs have been found in several gravesites. They may date to the time when the village people were suffering from the plagues that decimated the Native American populations in the 18th and 19th centuries.

Could Tsagigla'lal's powers have been used for either or both purposes? One thing that is not debated is the fact that worshippers visit her at Horsethief Lake today. Some visitors to the park hike the mile or so from the parking lot into the canyon to visit the many pieces of rock art cut and painted into the rock there. Some of these people have placed offerings at the foot of *She who watches*, such as shells filled with flowers, tobacco or other small items. Some people have performed more destructive rituals. Many decades in the past someone took several shots at some of the rock art. The bullet holes are still there.

More recently, people have added to the Native American designs. Someone painted stars and sun/moon designs on the rock faces. These people undoubtedly felt that they were expressing their religious rights. They did not understand the terrible insult that they were making to the Native Americans who originally made the designs, or their descendents. It is also a felony. Finally, it is the reason tourists are no longer allowed to walk up the trails alone. Since the defacement, park rangers conduct guided tours to the rock art site by appointment on Fridays and Saturdays.

The Oregon Vortex, (4303 Sardine Cr. Rd., Gold Hill, Oregon)

The Oregon Vortex is a location in southern Oregon, near Gold Hill, an early gold mining boomtown. According to local legends, the Native Americans who inhabited the area proclaimed the land of the Oregon Vortex forbidden ground because of the many strange things that happen there. The vortex itself is a circular piece of ground, 165 feet in diameter. At all times of year, wildlife such as birds and gophers are rarely found inside the circle. Trees growing within the vortex incline towards magnetic north. An English engineer named John Lister made this strange phenomenon famous.

Lister arrived in Oregon in 1929, to conduct mining surveys. When he arrived in Gold Hill, he discovered a dilapidated log cabin that had been an assay office for a turn of the century mining camp. Lister noticed some strange anomalies in the magnetic field around the old cabin. He felt that this field, or vortex of energies, went so far as to warp the fabric of space/time. He believed that within the vortex, space is actually compressed and the earth's gravitational field was also lower than normal.

At the time Lister was charting the Oregon Vortex, he set up displays outside and inside the boundaries to show observers its effects. This includes having two people of different heights standing on a concrete slab. One person is inside the vortex, the other person is outside. The person standing inside the vortex is always shorter than the person standing outside the vortex. When the two people change places, the person who was inside the vortex (and shorter) becomes taller than the person who was outside the vortex (and formerly taller).

There is a large collection of photographs in the Visitor's Center. They show strange light effects on film that were not visible to the photographer when the pictures were taken. According to the staff at the Oregon Vortex, this phenomenon is different than that encountered by visitors when they enter the old log cabin.

As an engineer, Lister was familiar with the effects that light and complex angles can have on people's vision. He set up a series of complex optical illusions inside the log cabin. These optical illusions include standing a broomstick upright at an angle, and rolling a bottle uphill, among many other visual effects. These illusions have been copied by numerous amusement parks since Lister's death in 1959.

Like many places in the Pacific Northwest, it is the person who made the Vortex famous that overshadows the place itself. Lister was as much a flamboyant showman as he was a serious scholar. His obituary in 1959 gives some of the credits he claimed. He was born in Scotland in 1886, the son of an English diplomat. He was raised in South Africa until he reached school age, when he returned to England to attend University. He received a Masters in Engineering, and attended the University of Glasgow, where he earned a Master of Arts. One of his schoolmates was Alexander Fleming, the discoverer of penicillin. After several years of study, Lister worked as a mining engineer. His travels eventually took him to Oregon, where he became absorbed in finding the "secret" of the vortex.

He carried out many experiments to document the strange visual and physical effects there. According to apocryphal stories, Lister kept a large notebook of photographs and diagrams. When he died, his son is supposed to have burned it, to ensure that his discoveries did not fall into the wrong hands. Other stories hold that his wife hid them. The notes may have been lost, an d may be waiting in some attic in Gold Hill right now. What has survived is a small publication for sale in the Visitor's Center.

His heirs at the Vortex have carried on Lister's legacy. While I was there, I received a well-practiced interpretive talk from one of the tour guides, who freely admitted that some of the visual effects were optical illusions. At the same time, she explained some of the visual effects that she said were not optical illusions in scientific terms, based on Einstein's theory of relativity. The staff have conducted their own experiments, such as placing watches in several locations inside and outside of the circle of the vortex, to see if time passes differently inside and outside of the circle. You will have to ask them about their results.

Skeptics would enjoy a visit to the Oregon Vortex to try and "discover" the secrets of some of the visual effects or explain the apparent expansion and contraction of people within the vortex. I have practiced with optical illusions myself over time. If all of the visual effects are a trick, they are very well done. If someone has an explanation, I would be interested in seeing how it was done myself.

Another interesting note about the Oregon Vortex; it is haunted. Several visitors to the Vortex have seen Lister, standing at the high end of the sloping floor of the old log cabin. He is usually seen resting against the wall, laughing and plucking his eyebrow. Visitors have asked the guide the identity of the man, who somehow got ahead of the tour. During one sighting, a tour guide looked inside the cabin, and saw the apparition as well. He recognized Lister from an old photograph. After the quick look, Lister disappeared. When the other guides looked inside, they did not see him. Anyone leaving the cabin by the back door would have been seen.

Sources Consulted
Books
Howard, Oliver Otis,
> 1907   *My Life and Experiences Among Our Hostile Indians*, A.D. Worthington & Co. Hartford, CN.

Periodicals
Arnold, Matther
> 22 November 1963   "Human tracks in Goose Lake lava uncovered again," *Skamania Pioneer*, Stevenson, WA.

Beck, Bob
> 6 October 1960   "Could footprints in lava have walked away?" *Columbian*, Vancouver, WA.

Gibbs, George
> 1955 - 1956   "Account of Indian Mythology in Oregon and Washington Territories". *Oregon Historical Quarterly* 56 (4): 293 - 325, 57 (2) p. 125 - 167, edited by Fila Clark.

Gwydir, R.D.
> 1965   "Prehistoric Spokane - An Indian legend". *Washington Historical Quarterly*, Vol. 1, no.3, p. 136-137. Washington University State Historical Society, Seattle.

Richards, Leverett
> No date, "Moccasin mystery," *The Oregonian*, Portland, OR.

Internet Resources
Crater Lake National Park, *www.halcyon.com/rdpayne/clmp*
Foxworthy and Hill "Crater Lake and Wizard Island," *whttp://vulcan.wr. usgs.gov/volcanoes/craterlake/*
Oregon Vortex*, www.oregonvortex.com*

Portland Basin

Battle Ground, Washington
The angry house owner (Private residence near 229th and NE Heission Road, Battle Ground, Washington)

This story concerns a small, yellow two-story house located just outside of Battle Ground. This house may not be standing when this book goes to press, since the owner plans to demolish it and subdivide the land into a new, upscale housing project. The original house was built in 1888, and was in the hands of the same family until recently. In 1994, Ray bought the house as a speculation. He knew property values would go up and he could subdivide the property into more house lots. Banking on future profits, he did not care that the house, which was a rental property, was vacant more often than it was occupied-until he met the real landlord.

Although Ray intended to demolish the house, he decided that it would be good if he did some renovation before renting it out again. The previous renters had left the place in a mess, so he decided to clean it first. After cleaning the second floor, Ray went outside to wash the upstairs windows. They were so filthy, that he had to apply a thick coat of soap to clean off the dirt. When he squeegeed off the soapy water, Ray nearly fell off the ladder in surprise. He was face to face with an old man, glaring out at him.

Ray slid down the ladder, but rather than running away, he ran inside the house. In a matter of a few seconds, he was on the second floor, ready to confront the old man. The upstairs bedroom was empty. So was the rest of the second floor. He went downstairs and looked through the entire house. He was surprised not to find anyone, since there was only one door into the house, the front door he had entered through. Ray mentally shrugged his shoulders. He convinced himself that he had not seen a stranger, but instead had seen his own reflection in the clean window. He climbed back up the ladder and began cleaning the window of the other bedroom.

When he washed off the second window, he saw the same old man staring out at him. Ray paused for a better look this time. The man was bald, dressed in coveralls and was definitely frowning at Ray. Again Ray ran into the house in the hopes of confronting the old man. Again, the house was empty. Ray believes that the man was the ghost of the original owner or his son. Both of them had lived and died in the house, years before. Ray believes that they know about his plans for the house, are unhappy and wanted him to know it. This warning did not change Ray's plans. The house is currently vacant, and waiting to be demolished.

Portland

The Heathman Hotel (1001 SW Broadway and Salmon, Portland, Oregon)

The Heathman Hotel, with its Italian Renaissance façade and gorgeous décor was built in 1927. It was not built as just a stopping point for travelers. It was meant to be a place for Portland's wealthy to congregate in a rich, cultured atmosphere. It was meant to be a showpiece for the world to see the financial and social prestige of Portland.

High Tea is still served every day at 2 P.M. in the magnificent eucalyptus-paneled Tea Court. This tradition has remained, along with other elements of its décor. The paintings that decorate the Heathman are classics, ranging from the works of 18th century European masters, to Andy Warhol silk-screens. The hotel was renovated in 1998, and unlike many renovations, the changes did not affect its status on the National Register of Historic Places. That may be why the resident ghosts remain.

Most of the paranormal activity in the hotel seems to

be centered around Room 703. No one has ever seen whoever, or whatever, has been occupying the room, but they see the effects. Many guests check into the room, unpack and go about their business. When they return, they sometimes find a half-filled glass of water placed on the desktop. Sometimes the chair at the desk has been shifted, as if someone moved it to sit down. At other times a towel in the bathroom is removed from the bar, and put on the counter, as if someone used it. Most guests call the front desk to complain. This is how the hotel staff knows that this has been going on for several years.

At first the guests blamed it on the staff. Part of the normal hotel housekeeping procedure is to have twice a day maid service. The hotel staff will also turn down the bedcovers for you as well. It was easy to believe that a careless maid made a mess, instead of cleaning up. The hotel staff blamed the mess on forgetful guests, or intruders who entered the room. This battle of supposition changed when the hotel installed electronic locks in each room.

The new locks record how many times a room has been entered, and at what time. Now when a guest in Room 703 calls the front desk and complains, the concierge is able to go up to the room and take a reading of how many times the door has been opened. In all of the strange cases reported by guests, the electronic record shows that no one has entered the room besides the guest.

In September of 1999, hotel staff received one explanation for the haunting in Room 703. A guest, who is also a psychic, talked to management after staying in Room 703. She informed them that she had seen a ghost standing at the foot of her bed. After walking around the hotel to check for auras, she concluded that the spirit energy was concentrated in a row, from room 303 to 1003. All of these rooms are located in a line, one on top of another. Her theory is that a guest of the hotel had committed suicide by jumping out of a window, and was haunting the rooms he passed on his way down to the ground.

An employee who has worked at the Heathman for over twenty years, told another chilling story. Before it's renovation, the Heathman had turned into little more than a rundown flophouse. One morning, this employee entered one of the "03" rooms with his passkey. He did this to check on a regular tenant. The tenant was an old, destitute blind man that all of the staff knew, but had not seen for some time. The employee found that the old man had committed suicide in his room a few days earlier. This may explain some of the happenings in that room, but it does not explain other, less defined incidents.

In the past, there were many seemingly unrelated strange incidents reported by both guests and staff. Many people have felt cold spots, or breezes pass around them as they walked down the hall. Other people have heard the sound of whispering voices in the same hallway. Then there is the sound of disembodied footsteps walking down the grand staircase. It seems that there is a lot to see, hear and feel at the Heathman.

The Interstate Traveler

Before the construction of Interstate Highway 5, Interstate Avenue was the road that connected Portland and Vancouver via the Interstate Bridge. I remember those trips, because my sisters and I would be looking for the 20+ foot high statue of Paul Bunyan, which stood at the intersection of Interstate and Denver Avenues. Since Interstate 5 was constructed, most people by-pass the old route. Many businesses that lined Interstate Avenue as well as the statue suffered from neglect after this change.

I still occasionally drive along Interstate Avenue when I head toward downtown Portland. The economy along Interstate 5 is improving now and Paul Bunyan received a new coat of paint a few years ago. I am still impressed with the statue. Far too many monuments of our childhood seem to shrink as we grow older. Paul still stands an impressive icon of the myth of timber that drew settlers to the Pacific Northwest. Not too far away from Paul Bunyan is the Interstate Bridge and our next ghost.

On some autumn evenings, a tall slender man wearing a black overcoat and felt hat has been seen walking south, along the Interstate Bridge... and disappearing. Could this be the shade of Vancouver's Mayor, Grover Percival? This is the same mayor who once took a walk onto the bridge in October of 1920... and disappeared. Mayor Percival had been seen earlier in the evening, walking around town, talking to passers-by in a normal manner. He was observed walking onto the bridge, and not returning. A search followed, but it was not until late November that his body was found, hanging on a tree on Hayden Island.

His death was declared a suicide. However there is no known reason for him to take his own life. Although there were rumors of foul play for political purposes, nothing was ever proven. Some people who have seen the ghost wonder if it is Grover Percival reenacting his past actions as he took the long walk along the bridge.

The John Palmer House (4314 N Miss, Portland, Oregon)

The John Palmer house is another fine Portland Victorian house that has been saved from demolition and turned into a Bed and Breakfast. Mary Sauter and her family have owned the bed and breakfast for several years. Soon after they took over the house they began hearing noises from the upper floors. This happened several times when the Sauter family was having a party in the downstairs. They heard footsteps above them, and their dog growled as its hair stood up on end. For some time, the alarm system in the upper floors would go off for no reason. Whenever they investigated, the upstairs would be empty. A psychic guest confided her impressions to Sauter.

She told Sauter that the ghost was a redheaded woman, associated with somel theatrical trunks left behind in the house. The ghost stayed on to watch over the house. She was concerned with any maintenance the building might need. Historical facts, as well as the types of disturbances Mary and her family suffered seemed to confirm this.

Sauter knew something about the family who purchased the house in 1907. A red-haired woman named Lotta was the head of the family. Lotta had been an opera singer who had lost her voice after a long career. She bought the house in 1907, as a kind of retirement home. Lotta still likes music. When people play the piano, Lotta comes downstairs and is heard moving around in the front hallway.

In the early 1990s, Lotta became very active. She was seen by members of the Sauter family, as well as guests. One of the Sauter children saw Lotta at the foot of the basement stairs. On another occasion, several guests were having tea on the main floor and saw a woman walk through the kitchen and then pass through the kitchen door. Although

most ghosts are not seen, but heard or felt, Lotta has been seen most frequently. True to her history though; Lotta is silent, no one has ever heard her voice.

When I spoke with Mrs. Sauter in 1999, she was too busy to discuss any recent ghostly activities. In early 2000, I visited the house and saw that there was a For Sale sign posted outside. It would probably be better not to contact them with any questions.

The Pied Cow Coffee House (3244 SE Belmont, Portland, Oregon)

The Pied Cow Coffee House was formerly named Buttertoes, and is located on Portland's historic Belmont Avenue. The residents of Belmont Avenue are successfully rejuvenating their Victorian neighborhood. The Pied Cow is one of these old homes, which has been converted into a restaurant.

The house was built in 1894, and one of its first tenants was a woman named Lydia. Not much is known about Lydia, which is surprising, considering she was supposed to have lived in the house for 25 years. Some people remember that she lived on the second floor, where she was seen, day after day, sitting in her rocking chair at one of the tower windows. After Lydia died in the 1920s, the house was sold to a number of people over several decades. At one time a fire gutted the back of the house.

In 1978, Carolyn Hulbert rented the building and converted it into a combination restaurant and boarding house. The restaurant occupied the first floor, while boarders lived on the second floor. Before the remodel, the second floor was reached by a set of inside stairs. After the remodel, she built a second set of stairs to the second floor outside the building. The inside stairs were blocked off and converted into the cash register station.

The restaurant customer seating is located below the second floor tower room, where Lydia lived. This may account for the paranormal activity in the restaurant. Many people working at the cash register station have felt a strange presence. One waitress quit after a short time because of it. Some mornings the staff opened the restaurant to find that the tables and chairs had been rearranged. Once Hulbert found that the morning mail had been picked up off the floor, sorted and laid out on the counter when she opened the doors.

The cook, Dwight Peterson, was alone in the kitchen when several muffin tins flew off a shelf. They moved through the air, about five feet and landed on the floor behind him. He pointed out that if they had just fallen off the counter, they would have landed on the floor near the counter, not several feet away. He often felt like someone was standing behind him. When he turned around, there would be no one there. Despite the oddity of this situation, he never felt threatened. He always believed that the presence was warm and friendly. He was not the only person who felt that Lydia was friendly.

The previous stories date from the 1970s through the early 1990s. Since that time Lydia seems to have been quiet. Carolyn Hulbert and Buttertoes have moved to a new location but the building remains, as a slightly different kind of coffee house.

It is hard to adequately describe the Pied Cow Coffeehouse's theme, since it does not seem to have one. The interior design is a mix of Victorian-Hindu-Bohemian. This comes from the original Victorian woodwork and chandeliers, the many Buddhist wall hangings, an odd mix of water color paintings, and beads. The menu lists several pages of unique teas, coffees, beers and wines as well as light food and deserts. The customers are an eclectic mix of New

Agers, Goths, and people who just like to hang out. All in all it's an interesting place.

There have been some other changes in the function of the restaurant. The cash station is now a kind of artistic sculpture niche, and is blocked by a small table. I watched several people sitting at that table. No one acted like they felt anything strange. I talked with two of the waitresses. One was surprised to learn there were ever any stories of ghosts associated with it. I asked to speak with the owners, who live on the second floor.

After leaving my card, the second waitress told her friend, "I didn't know about the house, but I always felt creepy out in the back yard. Where the old shed used to be."

This was the area where a fire had gutted the back of the building and any other structure that had adjoined the house. Nearby is a fenced off area that is used as outdoor seating in summer. When I visited later, a different waitress told me that the owner does not believe that the earlier stories are true because there have been no incidents in recent years. Lydia may now be at rest, or she may have followed Buttertoes to their new location.

The White Eagle Tavern (831 NE Russell, Portland, Oregon)

The hauntings continue at Portland's favorite haunted nightspot. In 1998, the White Eagle was sold to the McMenamins company after being owned by Chuck Hughes for nearly twenty years. Many stories that grew up around the White Eagle date to Hughes' ownership. Immediately after the sale there were several strange incidents, then the ghosts were quiet for several months. After summer began, the spirits became more active. Perhaps they waited to take the measure of the new owners. In the early weeks of July of 1999, the assistant manager, Jeff, and several other employees witnessed many strange events.

At various times when the bar is empty, employees will smell smoke. When they investigate, there is no evidence of a fire anywhere. It could be some kind of a short in the wiring, but again there was no interruption of power. In addition to the burning smell, they are sometimes assaulted by the overpowering odor of cheap perfume.

In the past, the women's restroom was the scene of several strange events. In the mornings, the bar staff will sometimes find toilet paper piled up on the floor as if someone had a toilet paper fight there the night before. On one occasion, a patron had a paper throwing fight with the woman in the stall next to her, only to find the stall empty when she got up and checked it.

During the summer of 1999, a patron was using the restroom when she heard the door open under the door of her stall, saw the shadow of a woman walk by. She did not see or hear the woman go into the adjoining stall. When she got up, the patron expected to see the person who had walked by the stall, standing at the sink. Instead the restroom was empty. She hurried out and told the bartender, who assured her that kind of thing happened regularly at the White Eagle.

I visited the White Eagle with a female friend in January of 2000. She knew that strange things had happened in the bathroom, but was not sure what exactly to expect. She was using the restroom when she heard a metallic snick. She thought someone had unlocked the stall door next to her. She was surprised because she could not see any feet in the stall next to her. There was no other sound. She looked around the stall and discovered that it was not the lock on the stall next door that had locked. She saw that *her* stall door had somehow unlocked itself.

The most interesting incidents have happened to the manager, Jeff. One afternoon he was standing just inside the kitchen area, counting tips. To his right was the stairway leading down to the basement. The basement has been a focus of strange activity in the past. Some time earlier, an employee had wedged a spare menu board between the right hand wall of the doorsill and the pipes an inch or two from the wall. For some reason, Jeff turned his head and looked at the stairway. He saw the menu board fly from its place, on the right side of the doorway, across the doorway, where it struck against the left-hand wall with a loud slap.

Jeff had always been skeptical about the past paranormal events at the White Eagle. He usually finds a rational explanation. This event has him stumped. He could see how the board may have become unbalanced and fallen to the floor. He cannot explain how it could have flown across the doorway. Another employee was standing at the bar several feet behind Jeff when this incident happened. She told me that she saw Jeff look down the stairway and then she heard the crashing noise. He turned to look at her with his face white as skim milk. She has never seen him look so alarmed before or since.

Jeff seems to have been singled out by the ghosts, or just has bad luck at the White Eagle. In November or December of 1999, he was closing for the night. He made several trips to the basement, carrying food items, which he placed in the large, walk-in freezer. Each time he went downstairs, he saw that the door to either the small freezer or refrigerator was open. Each time that he put the food in the large freezer, he closed the door of the other appliance before going upstairs for his next load. Each time he returned, the small freezer or refrigerator door was open again.

On the next to last trip, Jeff stopped and cursed the ghosts for interfering with his work. He slammed the refrigerator door shut and went upstairs for his last load of food. When he returned and entered the large freezer, a piece of ice fell from the ceiling and hit him in the head. It did not hurt, but it did let him know that the ghosts were offended that he did not want their help in putting things away.

Ridgefield, Washington
Nordic Church

There is a church in Ridgefield, located on Pioneer Avenue, west of the point where it intersects Main Street. The church looks a little dilapidated, but you can tell from its tall stained glass windows that once upon a time it had many generous parishioners. Some of who may still return to worship. The church was built after an influx of Nordic settlers into southwest Washington around the turn of the century. Many of these people-mostly Swedes settled in Venersberg, some-mostly Norwegians settled in Ridgefield.

One of the first things that these newcomers did to ensure their sense of community was to build their own church, which was used as a house of worship until quite recently. Many activities in Ridgefield revolved around the church. In the late 1970s a group of parishioners were standing near the altar, planning a community benefit in the privacy of the church. Suddenly there was a loud bang as the front door of the church was thrust open.

The disruption was bad enough, but the parishioners watched in amazement as a small group of men and women entered the church on their knees. The newcomers approached the front pews without looking at people who were already there. As the newcomers neared the altar, the first group of parishioners realized they were not walking on their knees. They were only visible from the knees up. It was as if they were walking on a floor that was nearly 18 inches below the present floor level. When the strange newcomers reached the altar, they disappeared.

The living parishioners left the church, barely taking time to close the door behind them. Afterward they speculated on the strange appearance of the "ghosts", as they began to call the disappearing strangers. They did a little research and found that when the settlers built the church, it was not set upon a permanent concrete foundation. Instead, the builders set the church on blocks of cedar wood. The old growth cedar held up for several decades before it began to rot away. It was not until the late 1960s or early 1970s that the building was jacked up, and a concrete foundation was poured underneath it. This raised the floor level about 18 inches above the original church floor. The frightened parishioners believe that they had the misfortune to see the spirits of past churchgoers, still walking on the original floor.

Vancouver
The Ghostly Guide of St John's Road

In many places of the Pacific Northwest it can be easy to tell if the road you are travelling on dates to Euro-American settlement or is much older. When the Pilgrims landed at Plymouth Rock, they brought a highly organized system of urban planning with them. They divided land into one mile by one mile squares, called Precincts or Sections. All urban areas within the section were divided into smaller and smaller squares. All main roads were laid out along these lines, east to west and north to south, regardless of the terrain. Sometimes settlement went so slowly that the roads drawn on the maps were not built for years or decades.

Native Americans had a different strategy when it came to their trails and paths. They hardly ever traveled in straight lines unless they were moving across flat, wide plains. They preferred to follow the contour of the land, moving in circles around high hills, paralleling rivers and streams for some distance until they could make a safe crossing. When their paths intersected with other trails, there might be as many as four or five trails meeting at one point.

When settling the northwest, many Euro-American settlers would follow these trails, widening them until they could support wagons and later automobiles. As time went by, the old trails were paved over and became rural highways. If you drive the roads of the Northwest today, the long and curved nature of these roads will clue you into their real age. Modern urban planners have a hard time joining modern roads with these long, winding roads.

St. John's Road runs for several miles from Vancouver, Washington, to Battle Ground. It is an ancient road. It even has a guardian spirit or two that may date from the prehistoric period. St John's Road runs through an area that is still known from the old-times as 'Minnehaha'. The later pioneers called it the Black Forest. The forest is gone now, but the area has avoided the urbanization that has come to characterize Clark County. Stories about the guardian describe it as a dark figure, that escorted people through the woods. When they left the woods, the figure vanished. This may be a remnant of a Native American guardian spirit. Another story dates this ghost to the late 19th century.

In 1942, many families, including my father's came to Vancouver to work in the Henry Kaiser Shipyards. Scott Moran's grandfather also came to work in the defense industry. Rather than settling close to the Columbia River, his grandfather, Mike, preferred the quiet farmland and marshes that dotted the Minnehaha area. Mike moved his family into a farmhouse near the junction of St. John's and 78th Street. One dark rainy night, shortly after moving in, he was surprised to see a light moving outside of his living room window. This was years before streetlights were installed on St. John's Road, so any light was easily seen.

Mike walked to the front window and looked out. He was amazed to see a small carriage or buggy, pulled by a single horse travelling north along the road. A single kerosene lantern hung from a pole tied to the buggy. This was the light, that had attracted Mike. A man sitting in the buggy guided the horse through the rain by the light of the lantern. Mike thought this was unusual, but guessed that it was one of the older farmers who preferred to drive a horse rather than a car. Even so, he became curious.

This was not the only time he saw the horse and buggy. He saw them several more times, but only at night, during rainstorms. This was unusual, because the typical farmer was home and in bed before dark. Several times after the buggy passed, Mike ran outside the house and tried to flag it down. Each time his cries to halt were ignored and he watched the buggy continue down the road. After a few moments, the light would vanish. When this happened, he walked down the road to the point where the light vanished. He did not find any evidence of man, horse or buggy. Eventually Mike asked some of the old-timers who lived along the road about the strange apparition.

After several conversations, a few of them finally admitted that they too had seen the phantom buggy and driver. Some even claimed that they recognized the man driving it. According to the old-timers, the man had been a doctor who served the neighborhood several decades before. One night he received a message that a patient needed immediate surgery. Despite a heavy rainstorm, the doctor hurried out to tend to his patient. Today the land near the intersection of St. John's Road and 78th Street is very wet, with many seasonal ponds and wetlands. A hundred years ago the area had many more wetlands and year-round ponds.

In the past, there were a series of wooden bridges on St. John's Road that crossed these wetlands. Because of his haste and the bad weather, the Doctor missed one of these bridges and drove his buggy into a rain-swollen pond. He and his overheated horse both drowned. Ever since, their ghosts have been seen, hurrying to an appointment they have already missed. Many of these kinds of ghosts seem to fade with time, and it has been several years since the cloaked figure or the phantom buggy have been seen along St. John's Road. Of course, the increased traffic and streetlights may have frightened them away. Never the less, the road itself has an eerie aura if you ever drive along it late at night. It is easy then to think about the other travelers who crossed the same path as yourself, a hundred years ago.

The Kiggins Theater (1011 Main Street, Vancouver, Washington)

The Kiggins Theater is the last remaining old-time movie theater in downtown Vancouver. When my father was a boy, there were four. Many people forget that "Ma Bell" was not the only monopoly broken up by the U.S. Government. In the early days of Hollywood, many studios had their own chain of theaters. These theaters showed only movies coming from the owner studios. In the turbulent entertainment period between the 1950s and early 1960s, television began to erode the base of customer support for movies. When the government broke up the movie theater/ studio chains, many film studios suffered or went broke.

Like ripples in a pond, this affected many already struggling movie theaters who were affiliated with the studios. The Kiggins, built in 1936 was one of these theaters. It was kept open from the 1960s through the mid 1990s through the force of will of its manager, Betty Ann Howard. Although she was able to keep it open, Howard was not able to compete for first run movies with the multiplex theaters that became popular in the 1980s. In 1996, the Kiggins closed its doors, not in preparation for demolition but to begin remodeling for re-opening. In keeping with studio policies, historic theaters to have better access to more recent movies as well as running classic movies.

In May of 1997, the Kiggins reopened for business under manager Gary Hubbard. It was not until after the remodel that he noticed anything strange. In November of 1997, he was in his office on the second floor, when he heard footsteps coming from the attic spaces above. He walked from his office into the hall to follow the sound of the footsteps above.

As he wandered down the hallway, he noticed that the footsteps were no longer meandering, they began to mirror his path. When he walked into the projection booth, he could hear the sound of the footsteps coming from the attic spaces, following his path. This was surprising, since there is a concrete wall in the attic that separates the portion of the attic above the projection booth from the attic space above the hallway. He left the projection booth and went back to his office. A few minutes later the lights in the projection booth, which he had locked, began to flicker on and off.

A month after the Kiggins re-opened, Hubbard went up to the projection booth to see if it was set up for the evening movie. He found that the sound system had been shut off, the projector settings had been changed and the film on the reel had been improperly rewound. He had set it up perfectly earlier in the evening, before he locked the booth and went to dinner. Hubbard had thought one of the employees had purposely vandalized the projection room, and fired him. After the incidents in November, Hubbard began to regret firing his assistant. In addition to the poltergeist in the attic and projection room there are phantom audience members as well.

Some movie patrons may be aware of the fact that theater staff will frequently stand in the rear of the theater. This is not just to watch a free movie; they are watching the audience to see if anyone gets up in the middle of the movie to visit the concession stand. At the Kiggins, they are watching for other things. Hubbard and several members of the staff frequently see a dark figure get up out of one of the seats, and walk to the rear of the theater. There are two main exit aisles in the theater, and the figure is usually sitting along the row farthest away from the lobby. They have watched the figure leave the seating area, walk up the aisle and turn into hallway leading to the lobby, and…disappear. This can happen three or four times a night.

Most people exit the theater as soon as the movie credits begin to roll. Some people remain behind, to read the movie credits. The theater staff has to chase these people out, after the lighting comes up. Every evening when the lights go up, the Kiggins staff looks for one particular couple. They are always seated at the far end of the theater, waiting and watching the blank screen. When the staff walks toward them to ask them to leave, the couple vanishes. No one has gotten close enough to them to make out any definite features. They have noticed that the man wears a hat and the woman has her hair up in an old fashioned style.

The Proebstel Fur Trapper (Vancouver, Washington)

In the late 19th century the Proebstel brothers all filed adjoining Land Claims along the Indian Trail that ran east from Vancouver. This trail cut through the network of plains that dotted the forests of southern Washington. That trail is now known as 4th Plain Boulevard. The Native Americans were followed by Hudson's Bay Company trappers, and later pioneers like the Proebstels, who settled on the outskirts of "civilized" land. One of the employees or first settlers may still walk the trail.

Cheryl Macabee lives on a small family ranch on land that was split off from one of the Proebstel brother's original land claim. The only reminder of the Proebstels in the area is a church and the old pioneer store (recently renamed.) Those buildings, and Cheryl's house, which was built by one of the early Proebstels. Although it has been remodeled and expanded, the original pioneer house is still recognizable.

I interviewed Cheryl in 1998, and she recounted some of the many strange things that have happened inside and outside the house. Inside the house she frequently hears footsteps on the second floor when she is in the living room.

This is in the oldest part of the house. She noticed that her many pets, including her barn/bobcat- mix cat will react to these sounds, so she knows that she is not just hearing things. There have been many other incidents and unexplained happenings inside the house but one incident, which happened outside is most extraordinary.

One summer afternoon, Cheryl standing on the front porch sorting through some boxes she had stored there. She was bent over for some time, taking inventory. When she straightened up, she glanced at her own dim reflection in the front window of the house. She did a double take and froze. Standing behind her was a man, wearing a heavy coat and top hat. She spun around to confront the man, only to see empty air. She turned back to look at the window.

In most hauntings, a visual apparition usually disappears at this point. In this case, the apparition remained for several moments for her to study. She saw that the man was bearded and his coat was either bear or elk skin. His top hat was not smooth, but had a rough texture. His pants were either heavy cotton or wool. To her, he looked like an authentic 19th century mountain man; right down to his beaver felt hat. He remained where he was, looking at her or rather through her.

Cheryl showed a lot of courage, standing on the porch, facing away from her ghost. She moved around a bit, to see if his reflection remained. It did. Based upon his height, relative to her own, she guessed that he was not standing on the porch, or on the ground next to the porch. The only way he could have been reflected at the angle she saw was if he was floating in the air, several inches above the porch floor. She could not resist the strain. She turned back around but could not see anything. When she turned back to the window, he was gone.

Was this one of the Proebstel brothers visiting his old house? Or was it a Hudson's Bay trapper, still walking the old trail? Was he standing on a phantom porch or a long vanished tree stump? Cheryl does not know. Whoever he was, he seems to be hanging around. She reported many other paranormal events in late 1999, but I will have to recount them in a later book.

The Slocum House Theater Co. (605 Esther St, Vancouver, Washington)

In the last months of 1999 and early weeks of the new Millennium, visitors and residents of Vancouver witnessed massive changes around the Slocum House, in Esther Short Park. The park is located in West Vancouver and is the target of a new urban renewal project. Fortunately, this time the Slocum house was not endangered.

In 1965, the Slocum house was threatened by an urban renewal project that resulted in the destruction of the many fine Victorian houses that used to line the old waterfront district of Vancouver. Fortunately the house was rescued by civic and preservation groups. They included many private citizens, the Fort Vancouver Historical Society, and surprisingly, a small group of citizens known as the Old Slocum House Theater Company. Since 1966 they have maintained the historic old building by using it as a theater.

Charles W. Slocum, an early settler in the Northwest, built the house. He was born in Massachusetts, one of nine children. Slocum's family were industrious Yankees who made their way as craftsmen, merchants and in various shipping endeavors. In 1857, twenty three year old Charles came to the Pacific Northwest, after completing an apprenticeship as a carpenter. He began working at the Vancouver barracks. In 1860 he opened a store and made a living, selling to the small number of settlers and soldiers at the Barracks. Hi business grew. His trade contacts ranged from Salt Lake City to San Francisco by the time he finally retired from business in 1890.

In 1867, Charles began work on his dream house. He based his home design on the house he grew up in New England. He and his brother did some of the fine carpentry work in the house. The most prominent feature of the house is the "widow's walk" tower that gave a spectacular view of the Columbia River, before it was moved to its present site.

The first haunting there is rather small and even amusing. A full time caretaker lives in a small apartment in the building. He cannot keep cereal boxes stored on top of the refrigerator. Strange as it may sound, the ghost there does not like to have anything placed on top of the appliance. Whenever the caretaker places anything there, (mostly cereal) and leaves the room for a few minutes, he finds the object on the floor when he returns. It is as if someone came along, reached up and swatted the boxes off the top of the refrigerator in anger or frustration.

Mrs Slocum's ghost may haunt the old building. Laura Slocum could not have children, which was one of her only true desires in life. She and Joshua both loved children and always welcomed the neighborhood kids with cookies and parties. Sometimes when there are children present in the house, such as during a children's play, people have reported feeling a presence in the house. A few people have reported seeing a misty figure, looking at the children.

One of the caretakers was taking a bath in spring of 2000. He left the bathroom door open. He was not worried, since he was alone in the house. From the bathtub he could see into the woman's costume room through the open door. He sat up in the tub when he saw what he thought were curtains on the wall rustling and billowing. Even though it alarmed him, he did not leave the comfort of his hot tub. He told his sister Rebecca about it later, and blamed the movement on a draft from the windows. Rebecca informed him that there were no curtains or windows in that room, just costumes. She suggested that what he really saw was the ghost of Mrs. Slocum moving around the room, brushing against the clothes hanging on the walls.

The haunting extends to the basement, which is not part of the original house. In April of 2000, Rebecca was in the basement looking for shoes and purses for one of the plays. She saw something move out of the corner of her eye. She turned to look at it directly. There was nothing there. She resumed sorting through the purses. She saw something move again, in a different place this time. Rats? No, it was too big, and high up in her field of vision. Again, when she looked directly at it, there was nothing there. She felt a growing feeling of menace and watchfulness around her.

A few minutes later, she went into a different room to look at hats. When she turned on the light, she saw a figure, which moved quickly to hide behind some furniture in the corner of the room. Rebecca paused for a moment, looking at the stacked furniture. If this were a stalker-type horror movie, she would have gone to the furniture to investigate. She has seen enough of those movies to know better. From where she was standing, she was sure that there was nothing hiding behind it, not anymore. She left immediately after that, forgetting her interest in hats.

The Vancouver Barracks
Building 875, the Howard House

The Howard House is named after Oliver Otis Howard, also known as O. O. Howard. Howard's military career is a strange mix of both violence and benevolence.

Howard graduated from West Point in 1854, which made him an outsider to many of the West Point graduates like Grant, Sheridan, Lee and Sherman, who served together in the Mexican American War in the late 1840s. These same men later became senior generals and enemies during the Civil War in the 1860s. Howard served as an "Indian fighter" during the Seminole Wars, where he forged friendships with his own circle of friends. After the end of the Seminole wars, Howard contemplated retiring from active duty.

At the beginning of the Civil War, Howard faced a choice between becoming a Gospel Minister or continuing to serve in the military. He resigned his commission as a Regular Army Captain, to become a colonel in a regiment of volunteers from Maine. He rose to the rank of Major General of Volunteers, after serving at the first battle of Bull Run and the Battle of Antietam. It was at the Battle of Seven Pines where he lost his right arm.

At the same time as he was directing battles, Howard was concerned for the medical and spiritual health of his soldiers. He tried making provision for church services and monitored the medical staff. A high point of Howard's career was during the first day of the Battle of Gettysburg, when he assumed overall command of the Union forces during the battle. After the war Howard continued to serve the War Department in a more civilian capacity.

Howard was a member, and once head of the Bureau of Freedmen, which was part of the Department of War. They were dedicated to ensuring equality between the races during the Reconstruction. In 1867, Howard and other liberals founded Howard University, near Washington D.C. The aim of the university was to promote the integration of African Americans into mainstream American society through biracial education. Howard's children were enrolled in classes when the university was first opened. In 1873, Howard was called to active duty where he became head of the Department of the Columbia.

Howard's command included Washington, Oregon, and parts of Alaska and Idaho. Although he was concerned with preserving the rights of the Native American's in the area, Howard was first and foremost a military commander. He ordered Native American leaders and their families held hostage. In June of 1877, many Nez Perce left their reservations in Idaho, due to a range war with Euro American ranchers. Their leader, Chief Joseph defeated a U.S. Army force at the Battle of White Bird. Chief Joseph fought Howard to a draw at the Battle of the Clearwater River, when Howard himself pursued Joseph.

Howard continued following the Nez Perce as they crossed from Idaho into Montana to join the Crow Indians. The Nez Perce split their forces and some of them crossed into Canada. Joseph and many of his followers stayed behind, where they sued for peace with General Howard. The United States Government, despite Howard's protests, did not follow the terms of the agreement. How hard Howard protested is still debated. Howard returned to the East Coast in 1880, where he became the commandant of the Military Academy of West Point.

The Howard House is named after Howard, because it was built as a residence for him in 1879. After Howard's time, there were several changes and remodels to the old building. In the 1960s the building was a non-commissioned officer's club and barber shop. A fire gutted the interior of the building in the 1980s and it was vacant for several years. Eventually the U.S. Army gave the building to the U.S. Park's Service, which formed a partnership with several preservation groups. After several major architectural changes, the building was opened as a visitor's center.

One of the major changes was the demolition and reconstruction an L-shaped wing on the right hand side of the main building. There are several historic displays in this new wing. In April of 1999, a strange thing happened to one of the exhibits. The exhibit, entitled "*One Place Across Time*", consisted of 20, four-foot by eight-foot glass panels depicting the history of Vancouver. On the morning of the 26th of April, a worker entered the building to find a panel depicting the Kaiser Shipyards shattered.

Charlene Dahlen, a representative of the Vancouver National Reserve Trust, jokingly suggested that the ghosts of the Howard House must have shattered the panel. When queried by the *Columbian* newspaper, she explained that it was not a serious comment, and they were searching for a reasonable explanation for the shattered panel. Eventually, through a process of elimination, civil engineers suggested that the new addition had settled, which put stress on the glass case. This in turn caused the glass to shatter.

According to a person who asked to remain anonymous, when the exhibit was installed in 1998, one of the glass panels shattered. At that time no one made any comment. They figured that this was just one of the things that happens when you move into a new building. After the second panel shattered, a worker went under the building and used wedges to re-level the building. A new panel was installed. The only problem is that later in the year… another panel shattered. After supposedly fixing the engineering problem, the building management has no reasonable explanation for these strange *coincidences*.

Nor do they have an explanation for the strange alarms recorded by the building's internal security system.

This system not only detects intruders, but can track them through the building. It records this information for later inspection by law enforcement authorities. There have been several incidents at night, when the alarm sensors have detected someone appearing in one of the second story rooms, in the front of the building. The intruder was monitored as they walked around the room, and then headed out into the hallway and down to a different room. This room overlooks the Barracks main parking lot. The intruder remains there for several minutes and then walks back into the first room and disappears again.

The security system has been inspected several times. There is nothing wrong with either the computer controlling it or the sensors placed throughout the building. It is interesting that several times in the past, people have seen a strange figure walking in the building while it was abandoned. One of these people include the ex-commander of the post. He was walking through the barracks one night in the early 1990s when he saw a ghostly figure silhouetted in one of the second story windows. He watched the figure moving back and forth between the two front rooms on the second floor. The Howard House was still vacant and covered with tarps and plywood.

A friend who works in a small shipwright facility in Camas recently contacted me. He spends a lot of time on sail powered ships. He has read my books and suggested that some of the strange occurrences at the Vancouver Barracks have been caused by vibrations from the propellers of the large ocean going ships that make their way up the Columbia. I honestly don't know if this could be the cause. Low level vibrations can cause strange reactions in human beings, including fear, anxiety and even hallucinations.

Volunteers and staff have been sworn to secrecy about the strange happenings at the Howard House. If any visitors ask about past or present hauntings the stories will be flatly denied… which probably means that this book will not be carried in their gift shop either.

Building 991 skeptics have pointed out that stories about haunted houses grow over time, particularly if the people who lived there tell their stories to new tenants. These stories grow, as they are passed from one person to another.

Sometimes when tenants change there is no contact between the old tenants and new. The stories are not passed on and the "haunting" ends. Skeptics love this, but hate to hear what happens in other cases. What happens when the stories are not passed from old residents to new ones, yet the hauntings continue, just as they had before? This is the case of Building 991 at the Vancouver Barracks.

This is the former post headquarters building, and was occupied by soldiers from the 104th Training Division until 1998. Soldiers from the 396th Field Hospital unit now occupy it. I visited the building early in 1999 to visit some friends who had been stationed in a base near my own in Bosnia, in 1997. I spoke with the unit's Chief Wardmaster, a kind of hospital bed/space manager, which is an imposing title for such a nice person.

I tried not to influence her when I asked if she or other soldiers had noticed any strange happenings after they moved into the building. Before they moved in, there were many incidents when the building was empty, except for a few full time employees on the ground floor. Around 4:30 P. M., the staff would hear the sound of someone walking down the stairs from the second floor to the main floor. The footsteps would continue down the hallway to exit via the front door. If one of the employees looked out of their offices to the stairs and hallway there would be no one there. Sometimes the disembodied footsteps would start outside the building. The front door would open and the footsteps would head upstairs. Again, when the employees investigated the second floor, there would be no one there.

When the 396th Hospital set up their operations in the building, everything was quiet for the first weekend drill. One evening after that, Sergeant June, the Wardmaster, was in her office on the second floor. She heard someone walk up the stairs, pass her office and continue into the open classroom that takes up most of the second floor. She was surprised because she was alone in the building, which was locked. She did not hear anyone unlock the door and come in. She was not thinking of ghosts when she left her office to look around. The building was empty.

Rather than panicking like many people would in her circumstances, Sergeant June shrugged and went back to work. She has spent several years working in civilian hospitals, and she has been stationed in many of the buildings at the barracks. Since many of those buildings were haunted, it was just another thing to get used to. Like some of the other paranormal incidents she told me about...

The Sentry

The parade ground located between the Vancouver Barracks and Officer's Row (the old military quarters) has become a favorite spot for people to jog, exercise or just come to enjoy wide open spaces. Many people have sought shelter from the intermittent rainstorms in the gazebo, located near the center of the parade grounds. The grounds have not always been as open as they are today. In the past there were several structures, including a sentry post and powder magazine in what is now an open field. It seems that some ghosts are tied to these vanished buildings.

In 1997 or 1998, a couple stopped on Officer's Row to walk on the parade grounds. They arrived near midnight but were not concerned at first. They had taken several nightly walks around the open spaces. That night the wind was blowing gently, as it sometimes does, but it felt somehow different to both of them. They stepped out of their car and began walking to the gazebo, when the woman told the man that she saw a man in an old style soldier's uniform.

The man did not see the soldier, but he heard a strange man's voice yelling at them. The soldier yelled, for them to leave the grounds of the post before he opened fire on them. The couple ran back to their car and jumped in. As they drove out of the parking lot they both saw a man in soldier's uniform watching them. He even tipped his hat at them as they pulled onto the main street.

West Linn, Oregon
The West Linn Paper Company (Moore Island, West Linn, Oregon)

In the 1850s, Robert Moore built a flour mill on Moore Island. The mill was a little too close to the high-water mark, because it washed away in the flood of 1861. A few years later, a second mill was constructed on the island. This time the builders excavated a large basement for storage from the solid rock of the island. This stone basement was an attractive feature for the paper mill that took over the facility when the flour mill shut down decades later. In 1889, the Willamette Pulp and Paper Company refurbished and reopened the facility as a paper mill. The basement was used as a storage facility for logs waiting to be cut.

The mill itself is the oldest operating sawmill in the Pacific Northwest. In 1920, the average laborer was paid 57 cents an hour. The plant manager was paid two hundred dollars a month and was provided with his own house and given three meals a day at the Company owned restaurant. The mill employed between 600 - 1100 workers, a much larger work force than today. In 1997, the mill became part of the West Linn Paper Company. With modern machines, the mill now employs 300 people.

Over the years, there were many technological changes at the old mill. The basement went from storage to processing. Log grinding rooms were built, where logs were machine ground into sawdust. Technology changed again, and the log grinding rooms are now vacant. Log Room Number Two may still have ghostly workers showing up for work, even though there are no more logs to grind.

Phil Peterson used to work for the West Linn Paper Company as part of the plant cleaning service. Peterson experienced chills more than once in the abandoned restroom in the basement, also called the catacombs. He stated that on several occasions he heard voices coming from the empty basement room. In one instance, he heard voices and got a security guard to go in the room with him. They both heard one male voice ask what time it was. They heard another voice reply that it was time to go home. Peterson looked at the clock on the wall, and sure enough, it read five o'clock. The problem was that the clock was not plugged in. How could it have read the correct time? He and the guard exchanged panicked looks and ran out of the basement.

In January of 2000, I spoke with a company representative about any stories other employees had about the old mill. Ian has worked for the company in human resources since 1985. He told me he had not heard any stories from people about groaning noises or clanking chains but admitted that fifteen years was not a long time with respect to a facility that is over 110 years old. Peterson hoped that the basement might be converted into a museum or interpretive center. A citizens advisory panel is discussing a new facility, but it does not seem likely that the old mill will be used.

Sources Consulted

Books
Howard, Oliver Otis,
  1907 *My Life and Experiences Among Our Hostile Indians*, A.D. Worthington & Co. Hartford, CN.
Jackson, Robert
  1992 *Great Mysteries*, Smithmark Publications, New York.

Periodicals
Cain, Chelsea
  October 1999 *Ghosts go bump in the night...,*" press release from Lane Marketing Communications, Portland, OR.
Clark County Genealogical Society,
  1989 *Clark County Pioneers.* Clark County Genealogical Society, Vancouver, WA p.292.
Erikson, Ruth F.
  1966 "Slocum House - 1966". *Clark County History*, Vol. 7, p. 142-145. Fort Vancouver Historical Society of Clark County, Inc., Vancouver, WA.
Hidden, Robert
  1965 "The Slocum House". *Clark County History*, Vol. 6, p. 69-72. Fort Vancouver Historical Society of Clark County, Inc., Vancouver, WA.
McCarthy, Dennis
  11 Feburary 1999 "Echoes of West Linn's Past," *The Oregonian*, Portland, OR.
Oppegaard, Bruce
  24 October 1999 "Downtown ghosts, as Halloween approaches, Clark County apparitions shadow our apprehensions," The *Columbian*, Vancouver, WA.
Thompson, Stephanie,
  5 May 1999 "Exhibit about Vancouver's history closed after panel of glass shatters," The *Columbian*, Vancouver, WA.

Internet Resources
Fort Vancouver Haunt *www.haunting.com*
West Linn Paper Company *www.wlinpco.com*
The Heathman Hotel *www.heathmanhotel.com*

Western Oregon

Ashland, Oregon

On my first visit to Ashland I stopped at a mall of small shops near Lithia Park. These small shops were located in one of the city's older buildings. Although the building is not impressive from the outside, it is nice and open on the inside. The first shop I went into was the "Witches" shop. One interesting feature of this shop is the floor, which is covered with coins. The owner does not keep a change drawer, so she prefers to leave it on the floor where it is easy to get to when she needs it.

I stayed there for several hours admiring the handicrafts on the walls and discussing local spiritual matters. Among the many things we talked about were the strange paranormal goings on, in and around Ashland. There are several groups of Druids, Wiccans and other New Age (and resurgent ancient) religious groups practicing in Ashland. Among other things, she told me about the cliff where several Native Americans committed suicide by jumping off while being pursued by attacking Army troops.

She also told me about the curse of Ashland. "One Indian told me that if you ever decide to stop here once, you will return until you finish whatever business drew you here."

This is not bad, as curses go. Depending on what brought you there in the first place. In my case, I returned in 1999 to gather more stories about the paranormal goings on for this book.

Southern Oregon University

Originally known as the Southern Oregon Normal school and later Southern Oregon State College (SOSC), Southern Oregon University is now Ashland's bastion of higher education. SOU began as a Normal school in 1926, and later became a women's school in the 1930s and early 1940s. After World War II, it greatly expanded its facilities as returning veterans took advantage of their GI Bill benefits. Like many colleges, there are several stories of ghosts and strange happenings on the SOU campus.

Many of these stories have grown over time and have passed into mythology. This process has been accelerated by the fact that most college students are on campus for four years. Their stories can grow more fantastic after the original experiencer has gone. This does not mean that many of the buildings are not haunted. As a matter of fact, some of the hauntings have continued for decades. The stories are remarkably similar, despite the fact that students have come and gone.

Britt Hall

Britt Hall is one of the University's older buildings. It resembles an old oil barrel, laid on its side, only it is three stories tall. The ghost associated with this building is unpleasant and elusive. Some people think that the ghost of an old janitor who worked at the university in the 1950s causes most of the strange happenings on the top floor and lecture hall. This janitor was a short, unpleasant middle-aged chain smoker with a raspy voice. While he was alive, he was repeatedly reprimanded for his attempts to have illicit contact with both male and female students.

Some students have seen him. They report being followed by a funny little man, who either scowls or reaches out to them as they walk by. Other students have not seen him, but they have heard the sound of his raspy, hacking, emphysema-labored breathing following them.

In the 1980s, a professor was giving a lecture in the large theater when he saw the heavy curtains surrounding him begin to ripple. At first he thought that wind currents caused the movement. He was surprised when he thought he saw the three-dimensional outline of a human head through the curtains, as if someone was hiding behind them. The head began moving toward him, under the curtain. The professor stopped his lecture and had his class leave the theater. It took a few minutes to empty the theater. When he investigated, there was no one there. There were no air vents that could have caused the strange movements of the curtains. There were two doors on either side of the curtain. However, both of these doors were locked. Could someone have slipped out of the curtains and left with the other students? Maybe; maybe not.

Churchill Hall
Churchill Hall is the finest building at Southern Oregon University. This brick structure was built in 1925, as the first permanent building for the Southern Oregon Normal School. The years have mellowed its outsides, with ivy trailing up its walls, and the tree lined walkway leading to its main doors. Churchill Hall is now used as a combination University headquarters and lecture facility. The University administrative offices are on the first floor, and a lecture facility with offices and large stage on the second floor.

Ghosts seem to haunt the upper story of Churchill Hall as well as they do Britt Hall. The ghost in Churchill Hall is more amusing than the sinister ghost of Britt Hall. This ghost inhabits the projection booth in the large lecture hall. On several occasions students and security guards have been on the stage when someone or something in the projection booth has made itself known.

In the 1980s, a group of students were on the stage

practicing a presentation in semi-darkness. One of them asked for someone to turn on the lights. The stage was almost immediately bathed in light, which came from a spotlight controlled from the projection booth. It took several moments for the students to realize that none of them had gone to the booth to turn on the spotlight. They ran from the stage, past the seats, to the ladder that led up to the projection booth. This is located in a hallway, behind the stadium seating for the lecture hall. When they reached the ladder they saw that the trapdoor that gave access to the projection booth was locked. They left immediately, without finishing their practice or asking for the light to be turned off.

A few years ago, a security guard was on a night patrol through the building. He stood on the stage surveying the lecture theater, with its several rows of stadium type seating rising above the stage. He glanced at the projection booth and froze. He saw a young man standing up inside the glass booth, staring at him. The figure was so lifelike that he called for back-up before he investigated. When the other security guards arrived, the first left the stage and ran up to the ladder, which is the only way into our out of the projection booth. As with the students before, the booth was locked. They had a pass key and opened the trap door. The booth was empty. If it was a burglar, how did he escape?

Plunkett Center, (originally known as the Chappel / Swedenburg House)

Plunkett Center is by far the most elegant

and homiest of all of the buildings on the SOU campus. It should be, since it began as the private residence of Charles Chappel, who later sold it to Dr. Francis Swedenburg, who maintained his house as a showcase of culture. It gradually fell into disrepair after his death and was later used as a dormitory. It was purchased by the college in 1965 and restored in the mid-1980s. After the remodel it was used as a museum and administrative offices. The museum display are now gone, but the SOU Alumni Association and Historical Society now uses it as offices.

The building achieved its chief fame as a haunted house in the 1970s. There had been some rumors of ghosts, but Professor Bill Muelemans, a security guard and three students wanted to confirm them. They held a vigil to see if the building was haunted. They brought a Ouiji Board, which gave several frightening responses to their questions. They ran out of the building in terror. The last person out, the security guard, was somehow stuck to the doorknob when he tried to close the door. After renovation in the 1980s, security guards were often called to the house by the new security alarm, only to find out that everything was alright.

For years after the 1970s incident, it was university policy that any students who were found on the wrap around porch at the Plunkett Center were expelled. This was done not so much to protect students from the paranormal, as to keep potential vandals away. After several years the ferocious penalty was relaxed, but the university and security guards still discouraged it. The security guards themselves do not like checking the building. They would sometimes find themselves watched by little old ladies, peering out through locked windows.

Portions of the building were set up as a museum, with period room displays. On some mornings, workers would see imprints on the beds, as if someone had spent the night lying on the bed. Many people have seen the phantom of a little girl in several locations within the house. By the time I visited in 1999, the paranormal incidents seem to have run down somewhat. Most of the employees I spoke with have felt a little strange, and some have heard what sounded like footsteps on the second floor. No one has seen anything strange in quite a while. Many of the museum displays have been removed to make room for more offices. Perhaps it was not the building that was haunted, but the furniture?

Suzanne Homes Residence Hall

When I first visited Ashland in 1997, the first reputedly haunted building I heard about was not Plunkett Center, but the Suzanne Homes Residence Hall. A student told me that Suzanne Homes was originally the town hospital. During the flu epidemics of the early 20th Century, it was overwhelmed with patients. There were so many sick and dead that the morgue was too full, and bodies were stored in rooms and hallways in the basement. Later, when the college acquired the building, it was converted into a residence, where a little boy drowned during renovations.

I found out that the first half of the story was not true. Suzanne Homes has never been a hospital. There is a grain of truth to parts of the legend. It was nicknamed "Suzy-Morgue" by students because when it was first built, Suzanne Homes was a twenty-four-hour, quiet dorm. There was a city hospital located on or near the site of the present building. It was demolished in the late 1920s or early 1930s when a larger hospital was built. The second half of the story about a little boy drowning is unfortunately true.

In the late 1940s, the campus was expanding quickly to support the veterans returning to school. Suzanne Homes was built in the early part of 1947. On the 25th of March, before the basement was finished, a seven-year-old boy named Donald Phillips carried a mattress down to the unfinished basement. He wanted to use the mattress as a raft to float across the twenty eight by one hundred fifteen-foot manmade lake under the building. No one knows how far he floated before the mattress sunk and little Donald drowned in the icy water. Since that time he, and perhaps other ghosts, have haunted the building.

According to one ex-student who lived in the basement of Suzanne Homes, she and others have been awakened at night by a knocking at their door. They opened their doors to find a dripping wet little boy, who complained of the cold. When they returned with a towel for the boy, all they found was a puddle of water in their doorway. Donald constantly plays with the bell attached to the door of student Kelly Harm's room. When she answers the door thinking she has a guest, there is no one there and the hallway was empty.

I visited Suzanne Homes in 1999 with Kaycee, a former resident. She told me of a storage room down the hallway from her own. According to campus legends, in the mid 1960s, a woman lived there, when it was an ordinary dorm room. She committed suicide in the room. It was left vacant until the next fall, when it was rented to another female student. The new resident lived in the room for a few weeks before she began suffering from severe depression; and later committed suicide!

After that the room was closed off and eventually turned into a utility room. When I visited, the room was open. It was filled with ordinary janitorial and maintenance equipment. How much truth is there to the legends? According to Kayce, there is a scrapbook that circulates throughout the dorm. It contains newspaper clippings and stories written about the goings on at Suzanne Homes. They include the stories about the suicides.

There are other strange stories about the Suzanne Holmes dormitory. On several occasions residents and security personnel have heard the piano on the first floor lounge play, even though there was no one sitting at it.

Dormitory rooms are found unlocked or open, even after their occupants made sure to lock them. Many people hear strange growling noises in the hallways at night, noises that could not be made by human throats. Could this be noise from the building's heating system, or something else?

Most SOU students are familiar with the fact that there is over a mile of tunnels running from building to building of the dispersed campus. This tunnel system contains the universities phone lines, fiber optic cable, power lines and the steam heating pipe from the main heating plant to the other buildings. The tunnel entrance door to Suzanne Homes is frequently found unlocked, which should not happen. In the early 1990s there was a rash of vandalism in the tunnels and campus security and maintenance staff have taken care to lock all doors to limit student access.

Once in 1998, Kayce and her friends found the door open and decided to walk a short distance down the tunnel. The tunnels are not cold and damp. They are hot and humid, especially in the winter, when the heating system is turned on high. They walked through spider webs in the dim light, up a flight of stairs to another door. They noticed an unusual feature at the end of the stairway. The stairs did not end at the door, but made a jog, turned to the right and continued up three more stairs, before ending at a solid concrete wall. Had there been another series of rooms, now blocked off?

The Watchman at Taylor and Central Halls

One characteristic of most hauntings is that ghosts seem to be tied to one location. This location is usually a single room where a tragedy took place, or even where the person who became the ghost spent a great deal of their time. Most ghosts do not seem aware that there has been a change to the building or that there are other people around. It is rare for a ghost to be aware of normal goings on and even rarer for them to move from one location to the next. The haunting at Central and Taylor Halls is one such example. It may not be too surprising, considering the identity of the ghost; a conscientious campus security guard.

This particular guard graduated from the University's Department of Criminal Justice in the 1960s and stayed on as a security employee. He worked at the university until he died in the 1980s. While he was alive, his favorite patrol beat was Taylor Hall, which was the home of the Criminology Department.

The day he died, the guard reported severe chest pains to his boss, and left work early to have it checked out. Later that evening a friends saw him walking down the hall, in uniform. He paused at her door, but instead of stopping to chat, he told her that he had to go but would be back later. A few minutes later, she received a phone call that informed her that her friend the guard, had died of a massive heart attack a few minutes earlier. About the same time she saw him. The guard was true to his word; he has been seen several times in both Taylor and Central Halls.

One day, a bored student named John decided to go through some of the storerooms in Taylor Hall. He liked looking through dusty closets, which is one of the first steps in becoming an archaeologist (John's major). His search was rewarded when he found a dusty photograph of a man standing in front of Taylor Hall. The man was wearing a security uniform, and holding up a diploma. John was surprised when something made him turn around, and he saw the same man, a little older but still in uniform, looking at him. The man did not look pleased.

The guard took the picture away from John, and politely asked him not to touch anything in the storage areas. He also politely asked John to leave because it was not safe. John mentioned the incident to his wife, a faculty member, later that day. She described the security guard to him, and John agreed it was the same man. He asked her if the guard was always so rude. She replied that he was only that way since his death. John encountered him at a later time, where the guard was still abrupt, but with good reason.

A few months later, John was in Taylor Hall, putting away Archaeology Club materials. The club's normal storage room, next to the basement boiler room, was locked. It was 11 P.M., and John wanted to go home. He saw that the boiler room door was ajar and the light was on. He had never liked the strange feelings he got when he was close to the boiler room, but was impatient to go home for the night. He carried the bags and boxes he was holding toward the room. Hopefully the janitor would be inside with a key to the regular storage room. At that worst, he might find some storage inside the boiler room.

John was within ten feet of the boiler room when he was assaulted by a wave of cold and menace. He froze with fear. The phantom security guard came up from behind and stood in front of him. He told John to put his things in his car, and get out of the basement. Now! The guard then walked into the boiler room and shut the door. John saw the sliver of light leaking form under the boiler room door disappear as the light was turned off. John made good time as he drove home.

John's wife, Jane, was a faculty member and her office was located in Central Hall. She had a habit of leaving her office door open, if she had errands somewhere else in the building. If she left her office at night to do something like get a drink of water, when she returned her office door was closed and usually locked. She assumed that a security guard closed the door on his rounds. One night she left her office, and found her door locked when she came back. Unfortunately, her purse and keys were locked inside. It was 10 P.M., and she was alone. She walked to the phones to call for help when she heard a man's voice behind her.

She turned and saw a middle-aged man wearing a

blue security uniform. He asked her if she needed inside her office. Jane responded that she did. The man took out a set of keys, opened Jane's office door and let her in. He tipped his hat to her and walked off on his rounds. Jane walked inside her office and turned to thank the man, but he had disappeared. A few hours later, she realized that there was something else strange. The man had been wearing a blue uniform. University security had changed to either brown or gray uniforms a decade earlier. After talking with several other faculty members she realized that many other people had seen the guard over the years.

Cave Junction, Oregon
The Oregon Caves Lodge (19000 Caves Highway, Cave Junction, Oregon)

In 1874, Elijah Davidson and his dog, Bruno, went hunting. The two chased a bear into a cave. Bruno was braver than smart when he followed the bear into the cave. Elijah followed after a few seconds, in the hopes of saving his dog. The historic record does not tell about either Bruno or the bear's fate. It does record Davidson's discovery. He found a intricate network of limestone caves, which takes up 480 acres of horizontal space, with several vertical levels. The poet, Joaquin Miller, called the cave the "Marble Halls of Oregon."

In 1909, President Taft declared the network of caves a national monument. The stalactite and stalagmite limestone formations within the cave resemble marble, in shapes like pipe organs, lotus flowers and even strips of bacon. It is appropriate that there is even a "ghost room." This chamber is two hundred fifty feet long, fifty feet wide, with forty foot high ceiling. It is called the ghost room because the formations there resemble robed figures. A good place to stay when visiting the caves is the Oregon Caves Lodge, located across the street from the cave entrance.

The Lodge is a ten-sided building, constructed in 1934. Many of the historic features of the lodge have been preserved through the years. The original 1930s coffee shop, with its U-shaped birch-wood counters is still in operation below the lobby. In the lobby itself, there is a large rectangular fireplace and huge round beams made from whole pine tree logs. In the dining room a stream of water from the cave has been diverted, to flow through and out of the building. In a picturesque place like this, guests should expect to see ghosts.

They are not disappointed. The employees at the historic Oregon Caves Lodge have been sworn to secrecy about the resident ghost, Elisabeth. It is a little difficult for them to keep mum about her sometimes, since Elisabeth is focused on making life hard for them.

According to the legend, several decades ago Elisabeth and her husband were honeymooning at the Lodge. Her husband did not wait to return from the honeymoon to become unfaithful when a pretty maid caught his eye. One afternoon, Elisabeth took a long walk on the trails around the lodge and her husband decided to stay behind. She returned early and surprised her husband in bed with the maid. Elisabeth was devastated. Later that night she locked herself in the bathroom and slit her wrists. Since that time Elisabeth has been active in many locations throughout the lodge.

Elisabeth has a tendency to pester female staff members. Several maids have complained that they cannot keep linen folded. When they wash towels and sheets, the maids always fold the dry linen. If they leave the room for a few minutes, they find the stacks of folded linen turned into heaps of wadded cloths when they return. In the kitchen, when female cooks turn off the gas stove when they close the kitchen, they frequently hear the sounds of the gas jets on full blast as they prepare to leave for the night. When this happens the first time, they think that they have forgotten to shut off the gas. They turn off the stove, only to hear the gas turned on again a few seconds later.

Elisabeth is supposed to have stayed in Room 308, and remained after her death. Some guests have reported an uneasy feeling when staying in there. Sometimes the guests seem to disturb Elisabeth as much as she bothers them. Many guests and housekeeping staff have heard the sound of someone pacing up and down the hallway outside Room 308 when it is occupied. The pacing usually ends around sunrise.

In June of 1997, a couple were staying overnight in a second floor room. The wife sensed something strange in their room, but her husband laughed at her fears. He laughed until he had to use the bathroom. After washing his hands, "John" turned the water off and turned to go. Suddenly the water turned itself on full blast. He quickly shut the water off again and when he turned to leave it turned itself on again. After that, the couple questioned the staff about any other strange doings. When they heard about the pacing outside of Room 308, they decided to investigate. They did not see or hear anything but the temperature dropped nearly 10 degrees, as they walked from the stairway to the hallway, outside of the haunted room. This is a strange coincidence, if coincidence it was, for a temperature drop like to happen in the middle of the month of June.

Crater Lake, Oregon
Crater Lake Lodge

Although Crater Lake Lodge and the Oregon Caves Resort are both on federal property, the same private contractor manages them. I wonder what they make of their luck in having two haunted properties to manage. The geologic history of Crater Lake has filled volumes of written history as well as Native American oral traditions (see

`Native American Spirits' at the beginning of this book). The construction of the lodge happened only seconds ago…in geologic terms, but that is long enough for it to accumulate its own store of ghostly lore.

Crater Lake lodge was built in 1915, and the huge log hotel was an immediate sensation because of its wild setting. Entertainment at the lodge consisted of athletic recreation, like hiking the trail around the rim of the crater or sailing on the deep blue waters of the lake. At the end of a long day, guests could return to the lodge and sit and listen to a piano player in the Lodge Grand Room. Or perhaps sit and play cards or chess, dwarfed by the pine tree trunks that were used as columns to support the high ceiling. Some people would have congregated around the huge basalt stone fireplace.

Unfortunately for the Lodge, the builders made some shortcuts when they built it. The Lodge was constructed without a stone or concrete foundation. They used logs instead. During the Great Depression the logs began rotting and no work was done to replace them. Over time, even the high beams of the roof began to sag under the annual covering of snow. The Lodge was condemned and closed in 1989. At the last minute, Congress was lobbied to provide moneys to renovate the decrepit structure. After six years of work, the Lodge was reopened in 1995.

A few years ago, one couple spent a few nights in the Lodge and had unusual experiences. They had never stayed there before, nor had they heard anything spooky or strange about the lodge. All the same, when they were shown to their room on the third floor of the west wing, both husband and wife felt a strange presence. They did not see or hear anything out of the ordinary, but both felt a frightening, overwhelming presence surrounding them. After a sleepless night, they demanded a new room for the next night.

The manager never admitted that there was anything strange or paranormal about the hotel. At the same time, he did not seem surprised at the request for a new room, nor did he ask for an explanation. Sometimes a lack of explanation rather than an admission of facts gives rise to stories.

Grant's Pass
The love of a jealous husband (Private residence, Grant's Pass, Oregon)

In the early 1990s, Sandy and her husband Don moved to Grant's Pass when his job offered him a promotion. Shortly after they arrived, Don was diagnosed as having terminal cancer. Sandy quit her job to provide at-home care for Don when he became too weak to work or move about. From the time he was diagnosed with cancer, it was two and a half years before he died. In the end, it was only the love that Sandy and Don shared that kept him alive.

Sandy could not tell her husband goodbye. A nurse who provided hospice to Don had seen many people linger. She told Sandy that Don stayed because he could not say goodbye either. It did not surprise Sandy that death could not keep Don away. Shortly after the funeral, she noticed that Don remained behind to look after her. Most of the time he was kind, though his jealously would sometimes show itself.

She remembers the way his ghost continued to show her tenderness. There were many nights when Sandy would feel an unseen hand caress her cheek in the middle of the night. Sometimes when she lay down to go to sleep, the bed covers would actually move around her body, as if to tuck her into bed. There were other occasions when she would feel his presence around, like a spiritual hug. Were the ghostly hugs just a case of wishful thinking on Sandy's part? Was she just afraid to let go of the memory of her husband until she found someone new? After a time, she decided it was time to move on and possibly find a new husband.

It may have been her imagination, but how would that

explain later events? Don had been possessively jealous as well as tender. Sandy remembers one evening when she exchanged email messages with a man she met online. Sandy was thinking about initiating a deeper relationship. She logged off her computer and went into the bathroom. She paused in front of a large bathroom mirror, when it fell on top of her. The mirror was heavy and it hurt her when it hit her. It had been securely fastened to the wall; and had never fallen off before. She knew that Don had made it fall.

Although she was frightened, Sandy was more angry than scared. She called out to his spirit. She reminded him that he was dead and she was alive. If he didn't like it, she would call their minister and have his spirit exorcised if he did not behave himself! And it worked. She still felt Don's presence around her, but it was more subdued. She continued seeking new relationships, but could tell when Don did not think that the prospective suitor was right for her.

A few years after Don's death, Sandy met a man named Nick. Don visited Sandy in a dream. She was sitting up in bed and Don was standing over her, dressed as he always was, in a business suit. Don told her she had found the right man, and it was time for him to move on. She felt rather than saw a vortex open up behind him. It seemed to swallow up her dead husband. When he was gone, she felt the warmth and energy that had surrounded her since Don's death, gradually fade away. It left her cold. This confirmed Sandy's belief that Nick was the right man to marry. She never felt Don's presence again, and thought that he had gone. It was not until later that she realized that Don was not quite completely gone.

In 1998, Sandy's daughter and granddaughter came to Grant's Pass for a visit. When Sandy was speaking with her daughter, her granddaughter wandered away. Her granddaughter returned a few minutes later and asked who the strange man sitting in the living room was? They ran into the living room to confront the intruder, only to find the room was empty and the front door locked. Sandy asked the little girl, to describe the man. Her description matched Sandy's dead husband, Don, right down to the business suit he always wore. This was remarkable, because the granddaughter had never seen her grandfather before, except as an infant.

After a long courtship, Sandy and Nick were married in November of 1999. They decided to make a videotape of the wedding using a camcorder that had belonged to Don. When Nick turned the camcorder on, it did not work. They had used it several times before without any problem. After the wedding, it began to work again without any problems or repairs. They guessed that although Don had recognized Nick as a suitable husband, he could not bear to have one of his prized possessions used in the wedding.

Sources Consulted

Books

Nelson, Nicholas
        1980   *Paradox*, New Horizon Publications, Summerland B.C.

Periodicals

Anderson, Hilda
        3 June 1999   "Weirdly beautiful Oregon Caves a treat for the imagination," *Seattle Post Intelligencer*, Seattle, WA.

Genett, Kara
        3 November 1997   "Campus legends say buildings have a history of haunts," *The Siskiyou*, p.7, Southern Oregon University, Ashland, OR.

Logson, Page
Unknown
        6 December 1959 "Obituary of John Lister," *Medford Mail Tribune*, Medford, OR.

Internet Resources

Oregon Caves *www.hevanet.com/heberb/reports*
Crater Lake Lodge *www.hevanet.com/heberb/reports*
The Oregon Vortex *www.oregonvortex.com*
Crater Lake Lodge Southern Oregon magazine, *www.so-oregon.com/lodging/craterlake*
Northwood, John, ghosts of SOU, *www.ghosthunter.org/chapters/oregon*

Western Washington & Puget Sound

Centralia

Lullaby and Goodnight? (residence on Plumb Street)

When Laura told me the story of the haunted house she lived in while at college, I asked her if any of the incidents ever frightened her. She is made of sterner stuff than most ghost-hosters are. She told me that all of the incidents were merely irritating. Even so, the things that happened at the old house on Plumb Street, in Centralia, would frighten most people.

In 1971, Laura and three of her college friends moved into an old, turn of the century house in Centralia. They were living at the height of the mythical golden age, in which to be a college student. Free love; free thinking and liberal education electives. They celebrated it by spending a lot of their time being tipsy. In-between student parties they studied hard... and noticed strange things about their house. They moved in late summer and first noticed sporadic strange events in the living room and kitchen. They periodically felt a presence and their two puppies reacted strangely, cowering away from something they could not see. The puppies were always kept in an outside pen at night. One morning the puppies were gone and were never seen again.

As summer turned into fall and then winter, the activity became more pronounced. They began to notice cold spots in various places around the house. It is normal to have drafts in an old house, but these spots are usually close to doors, windows and hallways. They are not found in closed spaces or in the center of a large room.

They began to hear the sound of a woman's voice, singing. The voice was crooning a lullaby, as if she was trying to sing a baby to sleep. Laura described it as pretty; in a hair-rising-on-the-back-of-your-neck kind of way! Laura was not even seriously frightened by the scratch.

One night, the living room light bulbs went out. Laura balanced on a chair, holding the hanging light fixture, while trying to change the light in the dark. She felt a burning sensation run down her arm. At first she thought she had been shocked, or something had fallen from the ceiling down her arm. She climbed off the chair and hurried into the kitchen to examine her arm. She was amazed to see four parallel scratch marks, like fingernail marks, running from her wrist to forearm. Her friends were amazed. None of them could have reached up and scratched her, because she was standing on a chair. They waited until dawn before they went back into the living room to change the light bulb.

Despite the scratch and the eerie singing, they stayed until 1972, when they all graduated from college and moved on to new colleges or jobs. I asked Laura why she did not move out after she was scratched. She told me that she was not frightened at being scratched, she was just irritated because she was hurt... even when she didn't do anything wrong.

The Olympic Club (112 N Tower Ave, Centralia, Washington)

I visited the Olympic Club in early 1999, while I was writing *Ghosts, Critters and Sacred Places of Washington and Oregon*. According to many of the employees I spoke with at that time, the ghosts had not been active recently. That changed in the months following my first visit. In July of 1999, I stopped in to see if there were any changes and to admire the tulip pattern, leaded glass lampshades in the bar.

Most bars open in the late afternoon or early evenings to serve their normal clientele. The Olympic opens a little early, because some of their teenage customers come to play pool in the alcohol-free portions of the establishment. One July morning, Lee Anne was the first person in the Olympic.

One of her duties were to put silverware on the tables, fill the salt and pepper shakers and light the small candles at each table and booth. She worked, starting at the front of the bar, finishing in the rear. Around 1030 A.M., she came to the last booth at the rear of the bar. She was surprised to find the candle on the table, already burning.

She stopped and looked at the candle, then looked around the building. She was alone in the bar. When confronted by the unexplained most people run away. Lee Anne tried looking at it logically. She worked the night before, and knew that the last customer left the Olympic at 3 A.M. The candle at the booth was a small one, and had burned down about one quarter of its length. She judged that it could not have been left burning all night. It would have to have been lit at 9 A.M., or 8 A.M. at the earliest.

Could someone have come in early, lit the candle and left it to frighten her? That did not make sense, because no one had discussed the ghost for several weeks. A practical joker would have set up the incident by mentioning it a day or two early. They would have been hiding in the restaurant to watch her discover the candle. She went through the building to make sure it was empty. It was. Having looked at the situation logically, Lee Anne considered the illogical: the ghost had struck again. She was ready to run but was saved, when the other employees arrived.

The ghost who haunts the Olympic may be that of a man named Louis Galba. In 1908, a boarding house stood on the site of the Olympic Club. Galba lived on the second floor of the original building. The building burned one night and Galba was trapped in his room. After being burned, Galba jumped from his window to the ground below. He broke several bones, suffered internal injuries and died several weeks later. This leap may be the reason why the ghost has an affinity for the staircase and upper deck of the Olympic Club. No one knows for sure how the candle was lit. Could it have been Galba himself or did the spirit of someone else with a love of fires remain behind?

Mossyrock (Private residence on Main Street in Mossyrock, Washington)

This house on Mossyrock's Main Street was built in the 1930s, and has seen many changes. It was built as a private residence, which it was for three decades, until the 1960s. At that time, it was converted into a restaurant by Laura's grandparents. Laura and her brother lived there in the late 1960s and early 1970s. In 1972, they sold it, and it was turned back into a residence. Within months of selling the house, the new owners approached Laura's grandparents and demanded that they reverse the sale and take the house back, because it was haunted!

Laura's grandmother was shocked. "They think the house is haunted" she told Laura later.

The truth was, Laura's grandparents had never lived in the building. When they turned the house into a restaurant, they lived in a small cottage behind the big house. Only Laura and her brother had lived in the building. She confessed to her grandmother, "Well Grandma...it *is* haunted," and she related her experiences.

Laura and her brother lived in an apartment constructed in the attic. There was a small sitting room at the head of the open attic stairway, on either side of the sitting room were two bedrooms. Laura's bedroom was located at the back of the attic. When they moved in, she knew immediately that there was a ghost in the house.

She has always had trouble sleeping in absolute darkness. In her bedroom, there was a small light fixture over her bed, that Laura turned on and off by a long string attached to a pull chain. Many nights she laid in bed, with the light on as she went to sleep. When she woke up, the light was turned off. Some nights as she lay there, she would close her eyes, but could not go to sleep. Suddenly there would be a click, and the light would turn off. She would sit upright in bed, and turn the light on... and look around her empty room. This happened several times, until one night.

That night, Laura was determined to find out what has happening. She lay down in bed with the light on and held onto the string attached to the light. She held the string taut; there was no slack in it. After several minutes of waiting she closed her eyes. She felt the string loosen, as if it were being pulled down from above. She heard a metallic click, and the string suddenly jumped tight in her hand again. She could tell, even with her eyes closed, that the light was now turned off. Someone or something had pulled the string above her hand and turned the light off.

She jumped out of bed and ran down the attic stairs in fear. She paused at the foot of the stairs on the main floor, and looked up at the attic. She saw a point of light grow near the back of the attic. The light grew and seemed to move closer to the head of the attic stairs. The light expanded and then coalesced into the shape of a transparent man, with a small child perched on his shoulder. He looked down at her. Laura ran out of the house into her grandparent's cottage. It was not until 1972, that Laura explained why she had asked to spend that night on their couch.

After the light incident, Laura switched bedrooms with her brother and slept in the front room. In winter they put a heavy carpet over the attic stairs, to stop drafts coming from the unheated ground floor. Late one night, Laura was awake, waiting for her brother to come home. She heard the front door open and listened to footsteps heading up the attic stairs. She heard a rustle as the rug was moved away from the stairs, and then replaced, and then listened to the echo of footsteps continuing toward her brother's bedroom. The bedroom door opened, then closed.

Laura was debating whether or not to get up or go to sleep when she heard the front door open again. The sounds she heard five minutes earlier were repeated again. The steps went up the attic stairs, the rug was moved, replaced and the footsteps continued to her brother's room. She told her brother of this strange time slip or echo later.

Every Sunday, Laura's grandparents closed the restaurant early. One afternoon Laura sat in the kitchen rather than going up to her bedroom. She was watching television and decided to get up to get a drink of water from the refrigerator. She stopped when she walked into a column of cold air. This was not a draft, since it did not move. Laura put her arm into it. The air inside it was cold and clammy. When she pulled her arm out, her hand came out wet. It was more interesting than frightening to her. She called a girlfriend over, and the two of them experimented with it for over an hour before this anomaly disappeared.

The whole story interested and amazed Laura's grandmother, but she still refused to return the money to the new owners.

Orcas Island

The Rosario Resort (1400 Rosario Way, Eastsound, Washington)

Robert Moran began construction of his retirement home, which is now known as the Rosario Resort, in 1904. Moran, then 46, was forced into early retirement by the stress of his work. He came to the Pacific Northwest in 1875, at the age of 17. A skilled machinist, he began working first at logging camps as a cook, and later opened a machine shop in Seattle. Using his shop as a base Moran found work repairing many of the steamships that plied the northern Pacific. He was lucky when the Yukon gold rush brought thousands of miners through Seattle, bringing a fleet of transport ships. As the business expanded, Moran sent for his brothers and formed a partnership with them.

Using his skill as a designer, Moran obtained the contract to build the battleship the U.S.S. Nebraska in his own shipyard. With this new work, Moran was able to expand his shipyards, which became the largest in the Pacific Northwest. Moran was also a leader in the community. He served two terms as Seattle's Mayor and became personal friends with John Muir, the founder of the Sierra Club.

With all of the stress of his business and political activities, Moran became very ill. His doctors told him that he would only live a few more years. In 1904, Moran decided to retire early and enjoy what time was left to him. He purchased 7,000 acres of land on Orcas Island and began building his retirement dream home, which he called Rosario. Moran wanted his house to outlive him.

The building foundations were cut sixteen feet down into solid bedrock not poured out of concrete. Moran used concrete for the walls of the fifty four-room mansion instead. Other elements of construction are reminiscent of naval architecture. The roof of the mansion is made of sheets of copper and the windowpanes are $7/8^{th}$-inch thick glass; strong enough to resist any storms that blow in from the sea. Exotic woods like Honduran mahogany and Indian teak were used for furniture, paneling and parquet floors throughout the mansion. The estate included its own power plant, machine shop, gardens, ponds and several other outbuildings.

Life in his new surroundings invigorated Moran. He donated 5,000 acres of his land to the state of Washington. It is now known as Moran State Park. Instead of living a few more, tired years, Moran lived another thirty years. He died in 1943, at the age of eighty-six. Before he died, in 1938 Moran sold Rosario to Donald Rheem.

Rheem was a wealthy industrialist and inventor. His fortune was based on one simple invention: the hot water heater. Rheem and his wife, Alice, owned the estate for 20 years and spent over a million dollars adding to and maintaining Rosario. Like many American nouveau riche, the Rheem's sometimes gave in to their impulses, to the shock of the old fashioned locals. Alice Rheem would sometimes drive her Harley Davidson motorcycle from the mansion into the nearby village of Eastside. She would go to the general store and play cards with some of the locals. Although it was unusual for women of the time to ride motorcycles, it was more unusual for them to wear red nightgowns on their motorcycles, like Alice did.

After the Rheem's tenure, the mansion and outbuildings were turned into a public resort in 1960. The new owners have made several additions, including a conference center, and more buildings and guest rooms. Whatever ghosts there are seem content to stay in the main building. Employees and guests have reported seeing strange shapes at night and most prominently they have reported hearing a woman wearing high-heeled shoes walk across the hardwood floors when the rooms are empty.

Some people believe that these are all manifestations of Alice Rheem's ghostly remains. There have been bizarre incidents that seem to fit her personality. In the mid-1980s an employee was staying overnight in one of the guest rooms. As she was falling asleep she saw a shadow cross the wall of the room. She turned on the light and did not see a person, but the shadow remained. It moved across the wall, as if someone unseen was coming toward her. She felt invisible fingers caress her hand. At that point, around midnight, she left. When she handed the room keys to the desk clerk he noted the time, around midnight but the story did not end.

The next morning the desk clerk checked-out a trio of entertainers who had stayed in the room the night before. They complained about the woman who stayed in the room next to theirs. This was the same room where the employee had been frightened out of around midnight. The guests complained that starting around or after midnight they heard the sound of passionate lovemaking coming from that room. It had kept them up all night long. It was rumored that Alice use to have affairs with many men when her husband was out. Perhaps she still does.

The maids at the Rosario in particular seem to be victims of practical jokes. One woman had just started working at the hotel and went into the laundry room to fill a mop bucket. She filled the bucket part way, turned off the water and left for some reason. When she returned, she found that the faucet had been turned back on and the sink was overflowing. When the angry maid confronted her surprised co-workers about the practical joke, they informed her that this was a normal occurrence. It seems that when she was alive Alice was constantly pestering the maids about keeping the mansion clean.

Olympia
The Evergreen Ballroom (9121 Pacific Ave, Olympia, WA)

Even though it has an Olympia address, the Evergreen Ballroom is located several miles away from Olympia's downtown. When it was constructed in 1917, that was the closest that most cities would allow such places to their centers. In the early 1900s, a movement of people convinced that jazz music and public dancing led to alcoholism and moral decay swept across America. They actively fought against opening places like the Evergreen. As long as the clubs were discreet, local governments tolerated them.

The Evergreen Ballroom was one of many of these clubs, which dotted the Pacific Northwest. Until the 1970s, it was part of an entertainment circuit that included the Evergreen, the Jantzen Beach Ballroom in Portland and the Evergreen Tianon Ballrooom in Seattle. In addition to music giants like Glen Miller and Elvis, many black performers like Little Richard, B.B. King and Fats Domino performed at the Evergreen. It was not until the late 1960s that blacks were allowed to perform at mainstream clubs and auditoriums.

People visiting the Evergreen Ballroom sometimes think that it was originally built as an airplane hanger, because of its barrel vault roof. In reality the ballroom was designed with the roof creating an acoustically perfect shell on the inside. This roof was probably added in 1932, when the club was remodeled. Over 140,000 board feet of lumber were used to expand Evergreen Hall, as it was known then, into the largest building in Olympia. The air conditioning was designed to keep the most energetic jitterbugs cool. A new woodworking product called plywood was used to panel the new walls. All at a cost of $15,000.

The ghost who haunts the Evergreen dates to this expansion. Everyone who works there knows about Mary, or Aunt Mary as some call her. There are several small wings built on the main auditorium. One of these, near the bar, was a combination office and apartment for the manager. Mary was one of the original managers and lived there for many years. After she died, guests and employees often saw her standing by the entrance to her old office. She does not move far from there, though she has sometimes been seen dancing by herself when the band played slow music.

The new owner, Steve, has not seen Mary yet. He believes in the possibility of her existence though. Steve has worked in the entertainment and casino business for many years and bought the Evergreen as an investment. He would like to restore the Evergreen to its former glory, by turning it into a combination casino and club. He has been actively promoting the many new acts playing the club and participated in many charity events. If he is successful, perhaps he will be able to restore the vaulted dome, and maybe, maybe once in a while play slow waltzes, which may bring Mary back?

McCleary Mansion (111 W 21st St, Olympia, WA)

The McCleary Mansion is now used as offices for the Building Association of Washington, and not open to the public. I include it because it is part of the saga of Henry McCleary, perhaps the most successful lumberman in Puget Sound.

McCleary came to the Northwest from Ohio in 1890. He began as a worker in other people's lumber mills but he had big dreams. In 1898, he bought a small stand of timber and began his own operation. He expanded and took over the Chehalis Door Company in 1907. Around 1910, the town of McCleary grew up around his mill works. McCleary used to subsidize his workers by giving them fruit trees if they settled in his town. McCleary retired from his business in 1942 and died in 1943, at the age of 82.

In 1932, While McCleary was at the height of his economic power, he and his wife Ada began construction on their mansion. The house took two years to build because everything had to be just right. Joseph Wohleb drew up the plans for the McCleary Mansion. He designed many of Olympia's finest buildings. The house is a superb example of English Renaissance style and included a billiard room downstairs, stained glass windows and lots of fine paneling from the McCleary mills. A fine garden with Cedars of

Lebanon was designed and planted. The will behind the construction of the Mansion was Ada Johnson McCleary, the political and social partner of their marriage.

Ada McCleary was active in many of the important social programs and causes of her time. She campaigned for the Red Cross to gather supplies in World War I. She was a member of the Daughters of the American Revolution and served as Vice President General from 1920 to 1923. She never forgot a favor or insult.

The official story told about the Mansion state that Henry McCleary used to fish with C. J. Lord, Olympia's powerful banker. Lord told Henry that he was going to build a new mansion. Henry told Lord that he could build a better one next door, as a bet. According to other rumors, when Henry was starting out in the lumber business, he went to Lord for a loan. Lord turned McCleary down, saying that he would never amount to anything. It took years of work for Henry and Ada to prove Lord wrong. Sadly, Ada McCleary died before she could move into her dream house.

After Henry's death, the mansion was subdivided into apartments and later into business and state offices. In 1992, Corrine Jackman worked for the Office of Archaeology and Historic Preservation. She was in her office on the first floor, and left her office to get some water. When she returned she saw a strange woman sitting on top of her desk. The woman was in her 30s, dressed in jeans, a sweater and penny loafers. Strangely, she appeared as a black and white image, instead of living color.

When Jackman entered her office, the woman turned to her with a look that seemed to be part fun, part embarrassment. Jackman asked the woman to leave, and the stranger disappeared. A few minutes later she felt the presence return. Others told her that a psychiatrist had used her office in the past. A female patient had committed suicide there a few years before.

In the late 1990s, an employee of the OAHP brought his daughter Julia to work, as part of the Take your Daughter to Work Day Program. One of Julia's jobs was to shelve books in the library. She was putting books and reports on the shelves, first one book, and then a second. Suddenly the second one fell off. She put it back. The first book fell off. She put it back, and the second book again fell off. Not wanting to play the game, Julia ran up to her father's office and told him what happened. He told her that everything was all right, that strange things happened all the time.

The building janitor reported hearing the sound of a woman's laughter echoing through the empty building many times. He and other employees reported that the toilet roll in the women's bathroom was found, unrolled after he had put a new one one the dispenser. Who is the female ghost?

After Ada's death, Henry moved into the mansion with his family. Some people believe that Ada's spirit moved in as well. Henry later married Hilda Simons, which may have upset Ada's spirit, and led to the hauntings. I'm sure she was upset when the mansion was converted into offices. Since the Building Industry Association moved in, all the ghosts seem to have quieted down. This may be because the BIA has taken great pains to restore the house to it's former glory, perhaps soothing at least one restless spirit.

Seattle
The Baltic Room (1207 Pine, Seattle, Washington)

The Baltic Room is located on Capitol Hill and overlooks the older parts of Seattle. It was built on the steep grade of Pine Street several decades ago. This has been enough time for it to accumulate at least two resident spirits. The first spirit is that of a young woman dressed in an evening gown that reminds the club bartender and piano player of styles worn in the 1930s. This female ghost has been seen most often standing in the corner of the balcony, overlooking club's the main room. Both the bartender and the piano player have seen a tall, willowy figure standing there during performances. Occasionally she moves down to the main floor. Perhaps she has been attracted to a certain song, because the bartender, Lorin French, believes that a ghostly audience applauded him once.

The second ghost that employees have seen is that of a man. He is dressed in a dark suit with baggy pants. He also wears a fedora hat, which causes some to believe that he dates to the same period as the woman. A few believe that this ghostly man is looking for the woman. No one has any definite theory as to who the two were in life.

Doc Maynard's and the Underground Tour, (610 1st St., Seattle, Washington)

Despite his name, Chris Grimm is a very friendly fellow. He follows his namesakes, the Brothers Grimm by helping document and repeat local folklore by working for the Seattle Underground Tours Company. He started working for Underground Tours founder, Bill Speidel, several years ago. He began working in the kitchen and is now one of the company managers. He has some strange tales to tell about his early years and more recent times.

The first job Chris had was to come in early and make soup for the morning tour crowd. Sometimes he was the first one in the building, and he would be alone for hours until the manager arrived. At that time, the kitchen was on the first floor in the back of the building. On many of those occasions he noticed a presence standing behind him. Sometimes he felt a dramatic drop in the temperature, which was strange, since he was standing over a hot stove. The oddest thing was the way items would move, on their own.

Like many kitchens, utensils were hung from the ceilings or walls. Sometimes the utensils would begin swinging from their hangers. Utensils like large spoons might lift partially off their wall hooks and slam back against the wall with a bang. Sometimes pans and food packages would fly from shelves onto the floor. Chris began looking for a rational explanation for this. He thought that he was going crazy, until another employee, Dana was present when it. He could not blame it on traffic vibrating the building, since there was virtually none at that time. Was it the tide?

The heavy tides in the Puget Sound are the reason why most of the toilets in Old Seattle's first floor buildings were elevated several feet above ground level. Exceptionally strong tides have caused many seemingly odd, ghostly phenomenon. This could have been a rational explanation, if this happened at the same time as the tide came in and faded away as the tide receded. It did not follow the tides. Chris found an easy way to stop the poltergeist in mid-bang. One morning the banging was especially loud. To calm his nerves, Chris turned the radio on, very loud. The banging kitchen utensils stopped, as if they had never been moving.

After that, the morning cooks did their work with the radio on. Chris moved to other duties and responsibilities, but the poltergeist continued to manifest itself occasionally in the kitchen. It did at least, until the growing popularity of the Underground Tours made it necessary for a massive remodel of Doc Maynard's in 1996. Since that time, all poltergeist activity seems to have ceased. Even so, the morning cooks still turn the radio up loud, just in case.

The Underground Ghost

While I was speaking with Chris Grimm about the ghost in Doc Maynard's, I asked him about the stories of a ghostly bank guard reported by guides and tourists on the Underground tours. (See *Ghosts, Critters and Sacred Places of Washington and Oregon*) Of course, Chris was familiar with the story; and the variations repeated by the tour guides.

He explained that depending on which guide conducts the tour; the story can vary somewhat in its details. As one of the oldest employees, he gave me "the true scoop".

The tours began by Bill Speidel over twenty five years ago have changed over time. As more buildings are renovated, their owners have put the underground levels to use, and the tour moved to different locations. Ten or fifteen years ago, the tours opened what the guides refer to as the *new section*, under the Denny and Yessler buildings. After that change, people began to see the apparition. Reports have varied over time. Some stories are of a man in uniform. The most common apparition people report seeing is that of a man in formal dress, including a top hat and cape. Was this the spirit of Yessler or Denny, returning from some ghostly formal ball? Or was it the spirit of a ghost, playing a role?

In addition to this mystery, there may have been a burial ground in the vicinity. To lay to rest any Native American spirits, they had a shaman conduct a clearing ceremony in the basement. Despite this, the formally dressed man is still sometimes seen. Or is it a bank guard?

The Mayflower Park Hotel (405 Olive Way, Seattle, Washington)

The Mayflower Park hotel is the oldest restored hotel in downtown Seattle. It was built in 1927 and originally called the Bergonian. It was designed and outfitted to remind visitors and guests of a small but luxurious Old World hotel. Like many hotels, the décor of the lobby gives guests the theme of the hotel. In the Lobby of the Mayflower Park, a 200 year old grandfather clock keeps time by the light of a five-tiered crystal chandelier and stained glass windows. In keeping with the refined and understated theme of the hotel, the ghosts here seem to be quiet and polite as well.

The ghosts were fairly discrete and quiet at the Mayflower until April of 1997. Three sets of guests stayed in

Room 1120 and told management of a ghost. They guests were unrelated and did not speak with each other before the incidents took place. This ghost did not do anything spectacular, but it did make itself felt as a presence in the room. In the case of all three visitations, the guests felt that the spirit was benign. Only one guest, a travelling Japanese businessman, insisted on a new room.

The hotel manager, Marc Nowak, took the complaints seriously. He spent the night in Room 1120 to see if he could feel the same gentle spirit. He did not report any ghostly activity or presence. Nevertheless, when interviewed by the *Seattle Times*, he was in the process of finding a psychic or paranormal investigator.

The OK Hotel and Café (212 Alaskan Way S., Seattle, WA) Many people who go through past-life regression therapy frequently recount being someone important or rich in a past life. If reincarnation is a reality, the law of averages says that we were not all rich or of noble birth in our past lives. More than likely, we were peasants or at best, servants or blue-collar workers.

The same thing goes for haunted houses. I enjoy visiting haunted mansions and upscale haunted restaurants for the architecture and fine foods. Have you noticed that everyone knows the identity of the ghost in these places? The rich builder. At the same time, aren't the poor just likely to become a ghost as the rich? Even more so, since they generally suffer more and have more hopes to be dashed than the rich. This leads me to the O.K. Hotel and Café.

I remember the day I visited the O.K. Café. The owner, Steve, was sweeping up the broken glass on the floor from the last night's business. He stopped and took the time to tell me about the history of the hotel and give me a tour of the upper floors. Steve bought the O.K. Hotel in 1988, but does not own the upper floors, which operated as a hotel from around the turn of the century until 1972.

The O.K. is known to some people as the Old Klondike Hotel. This may be due to the miners who stayed there, waiting for the regular steamboats headed for the Alaskan gold fields. Steve does not know much about the early history of the O.K., but has seen records dating to the 1940s. The hotel's clientele then was mostly dockworkers and ex-prisoners on parole from nearby Monroe penitentiary. The hotel had 200 rooms, which cost 35 cents a night for an 8 x 9 foot room and 50 cents a night for a double room. There were 25 rooms on each floor, with only one common bathroom on each floor. It was not the kind of place where people stayed while they were on their way up.

As time went on, the hotel became threadbare, like its clients. In the 1960s and 1970s, it became a haunt of drug addicts, hippies and a small number of pensioners who could not afford better. Some stayed until the hotel was closed. Eventually only the ground floor hotel lunch counter remained in operation. Of course, given the hardship and fears that most of the residents must have lived under for months or years, some of this seems to have been left behind.

As Steve and I talked, employees and customers began to drift in. Everyone seemed to have some kind of strange story, making the O.K. a candidate for Seattle's most haunted night spot. Steve and the others told me of various experiences and phenomenon.

People have seen transparent apparitions, they have felt strange presences and even been touched by invisible hands once or twice. There have been sudden temperature changes as well as many instances of ghostly sounds. Here are only a few stories.

One afternoon Steve was talking with an older couple from the Midwest. They came to Seattle to follow the trail an ancestor who had stayed at the O.K. in the past. They both left in a hurry when the wife saw an older couple walk down the stairs from the second floor, arm in arm. As they neared the foot of the stairs, the couple became transparent and disappeared. Even more frightening was the fact that her husband had not seen them at all.

Steve has an apartment on the second floor, above the café. Several times he has been awakened in the middle of the night by the sound of someone whistling in the bar space below his room. The O.K. is not located in the best of neighborhoods, so at first Steve used to hurry downstairs to confront what he thought was a whistling burglar. Each time he went downstairs, he found the bar dark and locked up tight. He does not bother checking anymore. Other employees verified some of their common experiences.

Pat seems to attract one of the ghosts. He has felt a presence behind him, and more than one employee has seen a shape they described as a black tornado following him. That may account for the glasses that seem to break around him.

Raymond was working late one night on the second floor. He was doing the books when all of the sudden, the room became freezing cold. The feeling of a presence and the sound of doors opening and closing outside the room accompanied this. He called it an early night.

Marcene is a regular customer at the O.K. She is a professional photographer who specializes in thematic portrait photo art. One afternoon she and a friend were on one of the upper floors taking photographs. She stood in the doorway of an empty room and looked out the window, across an open space of about 15 feet, into the window of another empty hotel room. She saw someone standing by the window of the other room, looking back at her. She walked across the room to the window, for a better look. She watched, as the figure became misty and disappeared. She never took her eyes off the figure, so it could not have been a person who ran away after being seen.

The O.K. is now a combination café, bar and art gallery. It has become so successful that Steve expanded the bar into the next door hardware store. When he remodeled, he left the original counter in place. He is experimenting with live bands playing a mix of modern music, jazz and alternative music. This attracts a wide variety of clientele, which ranges from dock workers to office workers.

The Sit & Spin Laundromat (2219 4th Ave, Seattle, Washington)

The Sit & Spin Laundromat is one of those eclectic kind of places that you may see portrayed on a sit-com, but never expect to see in real life. The Sit & Spin is a combination club and Laundromat. The laundry portion of the club is very small, and located in a small room, adjoining the main club. The main attraction is, of course, found in the club portion of the business.

In the "sit" portion of the Sit & Spin, the kitchen, offers a wide variety of amusements. There is an email service, a jukebox and live music many evenings for entertainment. The kitchen serves a variety of foods and drinks that range from sandwiches and pizza to coffees, microbrews, mixed cocktails and a wide variety of drinks. One special drink is the Cold Killer, made from a mix of orange, ginger and cayenne juices (served hot or cold). The club has a definite grunge look that contrasts with its linoleum floor and Formica-topped kitchen tables. This is all a far cry from its origins.

In the late 1920s, band leader, and later politician, Vic Meyers opened a jazz nightclub in the Sit & Spin building. He named it the Club Victor, after himself. Vic's rise to political power began as one of those political jokes that can turn actors into presidents. In 1932, a newspaperman suggested that Vic Meyers would make a better candidate then any of the politicians. Meyers was a favorite of the newspapermen. Flamboyant, fun and unapologetic, Meyers was as ready to laugh at himself as much as the news, even when his club was shut down as a public nuisance. The assistant city editor for the *Seattle Times*, Doug Welch, thought that Meyers could add a little color to the race.

Welch and several other newspaper spokesmen convinced Meyers that, it would be fun. Meyers campaigned with a vengeance, lampooning the politicians. He appeared at a candidate's debate dressed as Mahatma Gandhi, leading a goat. His campaign limousine was a beer truck. When Meyers ran out of gags and one liners, the press invented new ones for him. Somehow though, he began to take himself seriously. When he lost the campaign for mayor, he called for a recount. Even though he lost, he was sixth out of a total of ten candidates. It whetted his appetite.

A few months later he contacted the *Seattle Times* and asked them to support him in a bid for Governor. They turned him down flat; the joke was stale. An incensed Meyers drove down to Olympia where he planned to file as an independent candidate. He was shocked to find out that the filing fee was a hefty sixty dollars. He asked the elections clerk if there was a post with a cheaper filing fee. The clerk replied that it would cost only twelve dollars to run for Lieutenant Governor. Meyers told the clerk that although he could not spell lieutenant, he would run. Meyers was elected as the Democratic candidate for Lieutenant Governor and later beat his Republican opponent by 40,000 votes. Meyers is just the kind of ghost to enjoy the Sit and Spin.

The building was remodeled in the early 1990s and immediately seemed to attract an other-worldly crowd. During the opening night ceremonies, a man came in and told owner, Lisa Bonney, that he was ghost hunter. He offered to exorcise any spirits for around $200. She turned him away, but quickly came to regret it. As if remembering it's past as a jazz club, when the jukebox is put on random play, it always seems to play jazz music. The ice tea machine would turn itself on and brew a batch of tea all on its own. One employee I spoke with always felt a chill when she went into the back hallway by the bathroom.

One night one of the employees was cleaning the bathroom when he saw something out of the corner of his eye. He saw an apparition with no head vanish into a stall. In another appearance, a woman was performing on the small club stage when she became aware of a man standing on stage with her. She saw him out of the corner of her eye at first. The most notable thing about him was that was wearing an old fashioned hat. When she turned to look at him, there was no one there. No one in the audience saw the strange man. She was not the only one to see a man wearing a hat.

Lisa Bonney saw the ghostly gentleman. She was alone in the club's band room around 4 A.M. once. She did not suspect that anything was wrong, until she looked at the wall. The light was behind her and she could see her shadow and that of another person. Reflected in the wall she saw the shadow of a man wearing a large Fedora-type hat. Based on the shadow, he had to be standing behind her. She whirled around to face him, only to confront empty air.

Snohomish

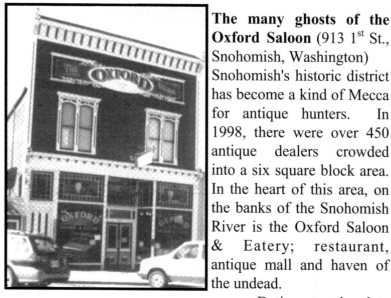

The many ghosts of the Oxford Saloon (913 1st St., Snohomish, Washington) Snohomish's historic district has become a kind of Mecca for antique hunters. In 1998, there were over 450 antique dealers crowded into a six square block area. In the heart of this area, on the banks of the Snohomish River is the Oxford Saloon & Eatery; restaurant, antique mall and haven of the undead.

Dating to the late 19th century, the Oxford Saloon had a checkered past. It has always been an eatery and bar but the upstairs was a combination rooming house and bordello. Many violent acts were performed there, but the most violent action center around the basement. The basement was used at times as a men's card room and bar. Local historians record several brawls, knifings and possible shootings happened there. Local psychic, Derienne Woogerd and the owner of the Oxford Saloon, Bill Mahoskey have detected at least eight spirits and perhaps many more crowding the Oxford.

The second floor of the Oxford Saloon is now used as offices and Madame Kathleen's Antiques. It was named after the famous Madame Kathleen, who ran the bordello there in the past. It is fitting that Kathleen is one of the more active ghosts in the building. She was forced into prostitution and hated her profession and her customers. Many men feel uncomfortable on the second floor and a few seem to be singled out for feelings of hatred directed at them. Kathleen has been seen by a few patrons. She is a middle-aged woman, usually wearing a long purple dress and a hat with purple bows and violets. She may also be the ghost that rearranges the antique women's clothing brought into the shop from time to time.

Two other female ghosts, known as Mary and Amelia may be responsible for the clothing being rearranged or moved. Mary was a bona fide boarder at the Oxford Saloon, rather than a "working girl." She seems confined to the room facing the main street. She has been seen several times as an older woman, dressed in a long, high-necked black dress. In life, Mary was jilted at the altar and ended up as an old maid, earning a living making handy-crafts. She is associated with a rocking chair and a blond china doll set up as a display.

Bill Mahoskey told me that the doll has a strange aura around it. It is attractive and has been sold many times. Each time, the buyer has returned it for one reason or another. Most of them admit that for some reason, it does not feel right when they get it home. Does Mary miss her plaything?

Next to Mary's room is Amelia's room. Amelia was one of Madame Kathleen's girls. If she did not love her life, she came to grips with it. Most people who detect her presence in her old room report a pleasant or restful aura there. Sometimes Mary is joined by John, one of Kathleen's regulars.

A male presence is seen in the upstairs from time to time. He is described as being of smaller than average height, with a full mustache and wearing a bowler hat. He seems to follow attractive women around the upstairs, following his usual practice upstairs. Witnesses may confuse him with Henry; a very active ghost show inhabits the first and basement floors.

Henry is extremely active and amorous. In many cases ghosts repeat the actions of their deaths. Henry seems an exception to this. He was a local policeman, who was a regular at the Oxford Saloon. No one has ever suggested that he was on the "take," but he may have been a regular at the saloon while he lived. One night Henry was called to the saloon to break up a fight. During the melee he was knifed, and died. Instead of suffering the same death trauma again and again, Henry has turned into a guardian spirit.

The basement still has a rough feel to it. It is too dark. There are pool tables and wood paneling lines the walls. Many customers have reported a watchful presence there. In addition to this watchfulness, Henry is more than a little bit amorous. Many women using the downstairs bathroom have complained to the management that an invisible hand has pinched them. A few have seen a man with dark hair and a mustache enter the bathroom after them, only to disappear when confronted. Bill was speaking with one of the witnesses on the first floor. She looked around the bar to see if she could find her masher. He was surprised when she pointed at a picture on the wall and told him that one of the men in the photograph was the man.

Bill surprised her, when he told her that man was dead. It was Henry. He is not confined to the basement either. In the late 1990s, Bill had a meeting with his beer distributor in the main room. The distributor was a very prim and proper lady, a contrast with the image of her beer. While they were talking, she screamed and jumped out of her chair. She had been pinched on the lower thigh. At first Bill was a little skeptical. To prove her point, she raised her skirt high enough to show him the red mark left behind by Henry's invisible fingers. Some people believe that this amorous behavior is not Henry's doing but is the work of the Oxford's original owner, Mr. Peterson. Peterson was known as something of a dirty old man in the years before his death.

In addition to the permanent guest ghosts at the Oxford Saloon there are several temporary ghosts that have found their way there. One ghost is named Simon. He died in a car wreck some time ago and has been seen on the second floor. A psychic told Bill that the souls of many people, both Native American and Euro-American are traveling toward the next life, following the course of the Snohomish River. The Oxford is located on the edge of a gully that used to feed the river. Some of the souls seem to travel up this dry streamlet, away from the river and find themselves at the Oxford... temporarily?

Whidbey Island

Whidbey Island, particularly northern Whidbey Island, might be better named Witch-bey Island, after the many strange and paranormal stories I encountered there.

A Native American people known as the Samish originally inhabited Whidbey Island. The Samish lived in villages, which they would periodically leave at regular intervals to hunt and gather various wild food crops. When Europeans arrived in the Pacific Northwest, they found the Samish involved in a struggle with the Haida people of Vancouver Island. Many Samish had died from European diseases, before the first ships of exploration arrived. The weakened Samish were preyed upon by the Haida, who raided their villages for slaves. For their part, although the Samish did not exactly welcome the Europeans with open arms, the Europeans were an improvement over the Haida, because they did not conduct slave raids.

Captain George Vancouver explored the Puget Sound in 1792, with his ship the HMS Discovery. Two of his officers, Lieutenant Joseph Whidbey, and Lieutenant Peter Puget spent several weeks exploring the land south of the Tacoma Narrows. At that time, they mapped the south coast of Whidbey Island. They thought it was a peninsula of land connected to the mainland. On June 4th, Whidbey left Everett harbor to explore northward. The tide carried his small boat through Deception Pass. This was dangerous for even a small boat due to the high winds and narrow channel in the Pass. When he exited the pass to the other side, Whidbey recognized the same land he had explored a few weeks before. The waters of Deception Pass are so treacherous, that sailing ships preferred to sail around the Island rather than through it. Until Captain George Coupe... *see the history of Coupeville.*

Coupeville

Coupeville is one of Washington's oldest towns, following in the tradition of Steilacoom and Vancouver. It began in 1852, when sea captains George Coupe, Howard Lovejoy and John Alexander began looking for a base of operations for their shipwright shops and homes, at the closest approach to the best harbor on Whidbey Island. They saw promise on the site of Coupeville, with its year-round harbor and the newly built Utsalady sawmill. Coupe himself is famous for sailing a fully rigged sailing ship through Deception Pass, on the north end of Whidbey Island on a bet. He is the only captain brave (or crazy, or drunk?) enough to ever do this.

By the late 1890s, Coupeville was a thriving metropolis. It had three hotels, a ferry to the Camano Islands, daily mail service, two churches, the Puget Sound Academy, a real estate office and a 500 foot long wharf, which allowed moorage for deep water ships. It also had *Magic Lantern* shows, the forerunner of the modern motion picture, on a regular basis. It recently hosted the film crew of a motion picture company. In the mid 1990s, scenes from the movie *Practical Magic* were filmed in Coupeville. The buildings in the town scenes were painted white, to simulate a New England fishing town. It is a bit disconcerting to see a block of solid white buildings set in the midst of the other multi-colored buildings of the town.

The Captain Whidbey Inn (2072 West Captain Whidbey Inn Road, Coupeville)

Its original owner, Lester Still, originally named the Captain Whidbey Inn the Whid-Isle Inn. In 1906, Still decided to capitalize on the large number of tourists who came to Whidbey Island from Seattle and Tacoma. He hired local builders, a father and son named Solid, to build a rustic hotel. Whether it was thrift on his part, or stubbornness, Still challenged the building skill of the Solids. Rather than importing fur or cedar wood to build the Inn, he had them build it from a large stand of madrona trees growing nearby. Because madrona does not grow straight for any significant length, the Solids were forced to build the walls in sections and then piece them together. This accounts for the strange yet pleasing log cabin look of the Inn.

The Inn was renamed the "Captain Whidbey" in the 1960s, by the new owners, the Colbys. Members and relatives of the Colby's have owned and run the Inn since that time. The present owner is John Stone; who also captain's the Cutty Sark, a fifty two foot ketch he charters for guests at the Captain Whidbey. In the thirty five years he has been at the Captain Whidbey, he has not seen a ghost and remains skeptical about it. He does admit that several guests and employees have reported seeing a ghostly woman in white, walking the halls at night.

The stories about this ghostly woman go back decades. Twenty years ago, a man stayed at the inn during the winter. He did not know it, but he was the only guest at the time. One night he left his room to use the bathroom down the hall. He was washing his hands, when he felt a presence behind him. He stepped out of the bathroom and saw a woman go into Room Number 8. The next morning, he asked the staff about the woman. They told him that he was alone in the inn and no one was staying in Room 8.

A few years ago, one of the housekeeping staff was walking down a pathway to clean one of the cabins. She was surprised to see a woman walking down the path ahead of her enter cabin that needed cleaning. When the housekeeper entered the cabin, it was empty. Since then, a woman dressed in white has passed many guests walking the hallways of the Captain Whidbey Inn. After walking by the guests, the woman simply disappears.

The children of the San De Fuca Schoolhouse (near the intersection of Zylsta Road and Highway 20, Coupeville, Washington)

The San De Fuca schoolhouse is also known as the Coupeville schoolhouse. In 1894, a special levy election was held to decide whether or not to pay $600 to purchase land, build and furnish a new schoolhouse. The turn out for the election was about the same as we find today. The levy passed, with nine yea votes and one vote against. The schoolhouse was built in 1895 and stands today, overlooking the intersection of Highway 20 and Zylstra Road. It has been converted into a private residence. This picturesque setting is the reason it was chosen as a site for a scene from the movie *The War of the Roses*. For fans of Danny DeVito and Michael Douglas, you will never see the schoolhouse, because they were not able to film this particular scene.

According to the story told me, the scene involved DeVito and Douglas sitting on the front steps of the schoolhouse, talking. The scene took two days to film because of technical difficulties. First there was a squeaking noise on the sound track, when there were no live sounds nearby.

Then there was the problem with the camera. For some reason, the electric motors that spin the film while the camera is recording would not stay at the correct speed. After numerous takes and two days of frustration, Danny DiVito is supposed to have stood up for a break and looked through the front door into the empty schoolhouse. After a few seconds, he turned around and remarked to the movie cast and crew that the place was haunted, and they were not coming back for a third day of shooting.

Movie stars are not the only people affected by the mischievous former students. The current resident of the old school is Susan Konopik. She runs a mobile massage therapy business out of her home. She did not believe in ghosts until after she moved in. She was making cookies in the kitchen, which had been the cloakroom. She turned around and saw a young boy with blond hair looking at her. She nodded at him, thinking he was a local boy who had wandered into the old school, then turned back around. She turned back to the boy, to offer him a cookie. In the second that it took her to get the cookie, he was gone.

She often hears the sound of children laughing for no

reason. Sometimes, when she is watching television she will hear girls voices imitating the voices on the TV. Whoever they are, they think that Susan should keep early hours. One morning as she was waking up, Susan heard several boys voices, whispering. They counted slowly "one... two... three!" and began yelling for her to wake up. Susan sat up and screamed back for them to shut-up. The yelling ceased. She looked around and saw that she was alone. The silence was more frightening than the yelling.

She hosted a Halloween party a few years ago and had several guests who did not know about the other *residents*. In the middle of the party the guests froze as they watched a glass bowl levitate into the air. After floating in place for a few seconds it hurled across the room and crashed to the floor. Most of the guests left quickly but the party lives on in local folklore. In addition to the bowl, other physical phenomenon includes the water faucets turning on and off when no one is near them.

A haunted mailbox? (located at a private residence on Zylstra Road)

I had a hard time with this story, until my friend Tony Popp explained it to me. People driving down Zylstra Road, near the San De Fuca Schoolhouse sometimes have to swerve to avoid driving over mail that has been thrown from a mailbox by unseen hands. The present resident watches the mailbox for vandals but has never seen anyone. He watches the mailman deliver the mail, and if he is not careful to keep his eyes on the box, sure enough, when he reaches the box, the mail is usually lying on the ground when he gets there. This ceases after a few days, only to begin again weeks later.

According to local stories, during World War II a husband and wife lived in the house. He was stationed at the Naval Air Base for several months until he received reassignment orders that sent him overseas. He used to write his wife frequently. After the war, he was not reassigned back to Whidbey Island, but to another duty station. He sent his wife several letters telling her he would send for her when the time was right. As time went by, the letters came less often, and eventually ceased to arrive at all.

The woman did not lose hope immediately. Every day she went down to the mailbox to check the mail for the all-important letter. This went on for weeks and then months until finally she gave up and left Whidbey Island. Whether she committed suicide or went on to better things, no one knows. Some of her anxiety seems to have been transferred to her old mailbox, and a part of her at least scans the incoming mail for the long awaited letter.

Oak Harbor

Oak Harbor was settled by Euro-Americans who moved in on the site of an already existing Native American village. This happened more often in the Westward Expansion than the Old West movies would have us believe. What was unusual in the case of Oak Harbor was that the early settlers, a handful of Irish émigrés, lived peacefully with the Native Americans. Perhaps that came from their own treatment in Ireland, where land clearances destroyed many of their villages. In keeping with their own traditions, the Irish named their town Oak Harbor, after a stand of Garry Oaks that covered the hillsides above the harbor.

In the late 1880s twenty Euro-American residents and an uncounted number of Native Americans lived there. In addition to the Irish, several Dutch farmers settled the land there as well. Part of the difficulty in settling the area was the fact that the railroad owned most of the free land and refused to sell. Even so, on July 4th, 1889 the town's inhabitants celebrated with their Native American comrades, who called it a *mamook muckamuck*, or work food. By 1892 the railroad began selling land, and the town began to grow.

T h e   H u r n Farmhouse (along Autl Field Road)

This house was vacant for years when I wrote the following story. Since I visited, it has undergone extensive renovations.

The Hurn house sits on a hill overlooking the Naval Air Station's Chief Petty Officer's Club on Autl Field Road. David Fischer owned the house and surrounding property. Although he never lived at the house, as a child he used to visit his friend Alan Hurn there. Alan used to tell David and the other kids at school strange stories about the house. He told of hearing people walking in the empty attic and the sound of disembodied laughing, late at night. Many locals who lived there told similar stories. Many people coming out of the CPO Club across the street have reported seeing lights in the house and hearing music late at night.

Jon and Laurie Arnott run the nearby business, Island Ink. They have heard stories about an old woman's ghost that haunts the house and plays a piano late at night. I visited the Hurn house in the summer of 1999. It was obvious that the house had been vandalized at least once in the past. Several of the windows were broken and the electricity utility fittings were removed. When I looked through a window on the south side of the building, I was surprised to see an upright piano in the living room. This leads to two interpretations of some of the ghost stories surrounding the house.

A reasonable explanation is that when the past residents moved out, they left the piano behind. Over the past decade and more, local teenagers have used the abandoned building as their party house. Since the electricity was turned off, they had to bring their own lanterns or candles. In addition to bringing in portable stereos, they would have probably played with the abandoned piano. This could explain the sound of music playing, strange lights and other noises late at night. On the other hand, some facts do not support this interpretation.

There are obvious indicators that can tell you where teenagers have been holding a drinking party. The biggest is the piles of beer cans; another is the other garbage and graffiti they leave behind. When I was there, I walked around the farmhouse. The first floor and land surrounding the house were relatively clean. There were no cans, bottles, food wrappers, graffiti or other evidence of late night partying. Then there is the presence of the piano. A piano is an expensive musical instrument. It is something that people do not usually leave behind when they move. Was this a case of the previous owner not having space in the moving van, or was the piano left behind for another reason?

As a postscript to this story, when I visited the Hurn house I took several pictures of the house. When I had the film developed, I saw two strange things on a picture looking inside through the broken south entrance window. In the lower left hand corner of the photograph there is a yellowish pink transparent discoloration. In the lower center of the picture is a misty white circle.

Both of these phenomena were not visible to me when I took the picture and yet were present on the negative. I took the film and negatives to the local photography store and asked them to examine my discovery. After 45 minutes of discussion, they could not find a reasonable explanation for either effect. This is significant, because for the first time in over 1000 photographs of haunted houses, I have a strange effect that I could not explain as natural phenomena or a developing error. *For a discussion of this photograph and ghost photography, please see Some Thoughts on Ghosts and Ghost Hunting near the end of this book.*

The lurker (Base Exchange building, Sea Plane Base, East of Oak Harbor)

Whidbey Island Naval Air Station has two facilities located a few miles apart on North Whidbey Island. This story comes from the Sea Plane Base.

When I go on a road trip, I usually have a location I want to investigate in mind. When I reach the location, other stories of nearby haunts sometimes leap out at me, as this story did. In 1999, I drove to Whidbey Island to talk with Tony Popp, who is on the staff of the *Whidbey News-Times*, the Naval Air Station's newspaper. Because I am in the Army Reserves I can stay in active duty military housing, on a space available basis. The housing facility is currently a group of nice, single-wide mobile homes, parked on what used to be the World War II Air Base runway.

When I checked in at the manager's office, I asked my question, "do you know of any haunted locations nearby?"

About 50% of the time when I ask this question, I am answered with blank stares or mumbles. About 25% of the time, people respond with accusatory replies of "Who told you that?!" The remaining 25% of the time I am rewarded with replies of, "Now that mention it, yes."

That is what happened here, but I was surprised at the site of the haunting. The clerk pointed out the window, at the Base Exchange, (or store). This building was constructed in 1942, as a hangar for the old P-3 flying boats used by the U. S. Navy. The P-3 had a large fuel tank, which made it an ideal aerial scout plane. Due to the importance of the P-3's role in the war in the Pacific, the hangar has been placed on the National Register of Historic Places. The changes to the hangar have been small, with new walls dividing the large inside space into a small snack bar, convenience-type food store, retail store and a few specialty shops.

The morning after my wife and I arrived, we walked across the tarmac from our trailer to the Base Exchange. It was 8:30 A.M. and we wanted to get breakfast at the coffee shop. As we approached the main entrance, we paused by a pair of tall garbage cans to look over the building. It is a large concrete cube, with a small pediment built over the entrance in an unsuccessful attempt to beautify it. After a pause, we walked toward the entrance. A man sitting on a bench outside the entrance called out to us, "You can't go in, it doesn't open until 9 A.M."

I have spent several years in the military and I identified this man by type. Many military people put in their twenty years of active service and retire, but still remain attached to the military life style. Once they retire, they find jobs on their favorite base as a janitor, cook or other job, just to stay around the military. I guessed that this man was just such a person. If I was right, he would know something about the haunting I had heard of.

"I understand some people think that this building is haunted," I began.

"Yep..." he replied.

"Have you heard or seen anything yourself?" I continued.

"Yep..." he replied again.

"Would you mind telling me about it for my book?" I finished.

"Nope..." he finally changed his answer. I was happy that he was willing to talk, but I wanted words of more than one syllable. I was rewarded when the man finally smiled, stood up and elaborated.

According to my new informant, who had worked in security and maintenance in the exchange, the building was indeed haunted. According to stories, in the late 1940s, one of the airplane mechanics walked into the propeller of one of the P-3's, and was promptly converted into a pink cloud. No one knows whether he did this on purpose or by accident. It is hard to imagine someone doing something like that accidentally. Maybe this is why he remained behind.

Over the past decades, many people have seen a strange man dressed in coveralls, walking along the catwalks in the warehouse portion of the hangar. When they climb up the catwalks to investigate, the man disappears. In most cases, he has been seen where there is no way a person could have climbed down from the catwalks without passing the people pursuing him. My informant once saw him, standing by the cables that controlled the hangar doors. That is another place where he could not have escaped. These doors were sealed when the hangar was turned into a store.

The ghost is active in other parts of the old hangar. In the morning when they open up, workers will sometimes find piles of clothing on the floors. Sometimes the clothing is arranged as if someone was wearing it, laid down and disappeared, leaving the clothing perfectly arranged; shoes, socks (with the feet inside the shoes), pants, underwear (inside the pants) and shirts. When this happens, the security system had not detected anything unusual the night before. Workers have heard the sound of footsteps walking through the clothing racks. The sight of clothing moving sometimes accompanies this sound, as if someone is brushing against the hanging clothes as they walk by the racks. Strangely enough, this ghost is accompanied by an unusual smell.

One of the ladies at the housing office told me about the haunted hangar. Her story was similar to my security guard informant's. It included an unusual detail about smell. Sometimes when they opened the store in the morning several workers noticed the strong smell of popcorn (buttered popcorn). The scent filled the entire building. There were no stores in the building that sold popcorn. Once this same woman helped close the building the night before and none of the workers had made popcorn in the employee lounge.

One of the responsibilities of the assistant manager of the Base Exchange is to lock the doors every night. As I explained earlier, the old hangar building is divided into several different stores. A sturdy chain with a key padlock secures the main retail outlet doors. Several times the manager and at least one other employee have closed the exchange, locked the door and walked away. They pause after they hear a clank and rattle, as the lock somehow unlocks itself and falls off the chain onto the floor. This has happened more than once. One evening they called the base security officer who tried securing the door with the same results. No one, not even the most skeptical employee, can explain the popcorn smell or the unlocking lock.

The Base Exchange is also the site of one of the strange events that happens to me from time to time in haunted locations. When I first began talking with the security guard in front of the Exchange, I pulled out the little writing pad I carry with me. I had trouble holding it as I wrote, so I decided to place it on the garbage can I was standing next to. I looked down at the lid of the can, to make sure that there was no gum or more disgusting "stuff" that might attach itself to my pad. It was clean. I placed my pad down and wrote for several minutes. When I finished writing, I picked up my pad and glanced down at the garbage can lid again. I was surprised to see a 1947 penny resting on the spot where I had placed my writing pad!

No one seemed to know for sure when the man had died, but the building was only used as a hangar from 1942 to 1951. The stories placed the man as dying sometime in the late 1940s. Could this have been some kind of ghostly effect, called an apport? An apport is a physical object that moves from one place only to appear in another by paranormal means. Since this a rare phenomenon, I immediately became suspicious.

Could the man have put it there to make the story more dramatic? This was unlikely, since he had not been closer than three feet away from me while I was writing. Could it have been a coincidence? Had someone picked up the penny, and rather than putting it in their pocket, left it on the top of the garbage can? Perhaps, but a 1947 penny has some numinastic value, and the first impulse of most people would be to put it in their pocket rather than to give it away. The clincher came when I talked the matter over with my wife.

When I moved to put my pad on the garbage can lid, she had glanced at it as well. She did not fancy having to listen to me complain about getting garbage on my pad. Just as I had, she did not see anything on the lid before I put the pad down. Neither one of us would swear in court, but both of us are reasonably certain that the penny was **not** there before I put my pad down.

Later, when I asked Tony Popp about the history of the Base Exchange, he was intrigued by our story. He did some research into the history of the building and forwarded it to me. He did not find any records of a deaths when it was a hangar but that does not mean they did not happen. I still have the penny and a lot of questions.

Sources Consulted
Books
Cook, Jimmie Jean
    1985 *A particular friend, Penn's Cove*, Island county Historical Society, Coupeville, WA.
Kellogg, Alice
    1946 An introduction to some of the First Seafaring Men on Whidbey Island, Whidbey Island Chapter #6, The Daughters of the Pioneers of Washington
Neil, Dorthy
    1993a *De Ja Views Historical Pictorial of Whidbey Island*, Island Images, Inc., Oak Harbor, WA.
    1993b *The Dutch Book, Celebrating 100 years on Whidbey*

Island, Island Images, Inc., Oak Harbor, WA.
Speidel, William
      1972?   *Sons of the Profits*,
Unknown
      1993   *Sails, Steamships and Sea Captains*, Island County Historical Society, Coupeville, WA.

Periodicals
Carbone, Vic
      October 1998   "Something strange - The haunted clubs of Seattle," *The Stranger*, Seattle.
Robinson, Kathryn
      3 October 1987   "Seeking the urban ghost," *Seattle Weekly*, p46.
Godden, Jean
      13 April 1997   "Freeloading guests at the mayflower Park Hotel," *Seattle Times*, Seattle.
Robinson, Kathryn
      28 October 1987 "Seattle spirits," *Seattle Weekly*, p36
Samuelson, Darren
      29 October 1999 "There's something strange in your neighborhood," *The Olympian*, p. 15, Weekend Stensland, Jessie
      31 October 1998 "The ghosts of Whidbey Island", the *Whidbey News-Times*, Whidbey Island Naval Air Station.
Taylor, Lewis
      5 June 1998   "Evergreen Ballroom has brand-new style," *The Olympian*, Weekend Plus.

Internet Sources
Vic   Meyers: *www.ktpl.lib.wa.us/v2/NWRoom/MORGAN/MORGAN/ Meyers.html*
www.captainwhidbey.com
www.mayflowerpark.com
www.oxfordsaloon.com
www.plaidnet.com
www.RosarioResort.com
Rosario, Mayflower Park Hotels, *www.nthp.org*

The Northwest Coast

Canon Beach, Oregon

Indian Beach, (Ecola State Park, near Canon Beach, Oregon)

If you look in a map of the Oregon Coast you will have a hard time finding Indian Beach. It is located in Ecola State Park and is now a picnic area for tourists. I speculate about whether or not there was a larger Native American population who lived there and are now vanished.

Before the time of Columbus, the Native American population of the Washington and Oregon coasts probably numbered in the millions. When the ships of exploration traveled by the mouth of the Columbia River, sailors noted the presence of hundreds of bodies floating out to sea-The victims of a plague? The only thing that may remain of the past inhabitants of Indian Beach is one map notation and perhaps a guardian spirit or two.

At least one group of hikers has had a strange encounter along the trail that passes Indian Beach. In the mid-1990s a teenager and his aunt were hiking up a trail. It went north from Indian Beach, high up along the face of the mountain that overlooked the ocean. At one point the trail was very narrow and enclosed by dense brush and trees. It was only open outward along the side of the mountain overlooking the ocean. The hikers stopped to admire the sunset for several minutes, then turned to continue walking up along the trail. They were surprised to see a couple walking up the trail a few feet ahead of them.

The boy and his aunt were surprised because it seemed unlikely that the couple could have stepped off the trail and gone around them. They called out to the couple, who were walking hand in hand, and asked for the time. The people stopped turned and told them the time, 3:15 P.M.

The teenager turned to his Aunt and suggested that they return to the beach. When they turned around to thank the couple, they had vanished. The two of them were curious about whether or not the couple had vanished like spirits, or had hurried up the trail, out of sight. They walked up the trail and headed around a bend, only to nearly fall over a drop-off, where the trail ended, hundreds of feet down into the ocean.

Did the couple walk up the trail and fall into the ocean? That seemed to be the only other explanation for their disappearance, unless they were ghosts. The man and woman had seemed ordinary, solid people, wearing contemporary dress.

Even so, the boy and his aunt were convinced that the couple had not doubled back around them, nor had they jumped off the cliff face. They turned around and stumbled down the trail in terror. A few minutes later, when they returned to the trailhead, worried relatives informed them that it was after 5:30 P.M.. Where had the time gone?

I visited Seaside, Oregon, in August of 1999. I stopped at the Chamber of Commerce to get a roadmap and directions. I wanted to take a picture of the Tillamook Head Lighthouse, and felt that they would know the best location for a picture. That day, the person on staff was a woman who had lived in Seaside for forty years. She gave me a strip map of Ecola State Park, and suggested Indian Beach as a possible location for a photograph.

I asked the woman if there was a hiking trail at the Park. Yes, there was, it ran from Indian Beach, north to Seaside. I asked her if there had ever been a landslide that had destroyed a portion of the trail. She seemed surprised at my question and told me that yes indeed, a landslide that had closed off the trail. In the late 1980s the whole face of the mountain north of Indian Beach had fallen into the sea, where it formed a kind of natural jetty. This lasted for a year, until winter storms broke it up and pulled it out to sea. The trail was closed for over a year, before it was reconstructed. All of this happened before the teenager and his aunt took their near fatal trip on the Indian Beach Trail.

There were two mysteries here. The first was the couple, and the second, where had the two hours gone? Was this a strange episode of lost time, where two separate groups of hikers has somehow intruded into the same space and time for a short while? Or had the couple died when hiking along the trail in the past and came back to warn others of the danger?

Newport, Oregon
Yaquina Head Lighthouse (Four miles north of Newport, Oregon)

The beacon of the Yaquina Head Lighthouse operates at an elevation of 167 feet above the ocean beaches. It shines from the top of the eighty-three foot-high tower, built on an 84 foot high rock face.

This high elevation led to stories and legends about whether or not this lighthouse was constructed at this point by accident or design.

According to one

legend, a lighthouse was supposed to be built on Cape Foulweather, but the engineers did not like the look of the 100+ foot high cliffs they would have had to scale to ferry supplies up to build the lighthouse. Instead, they opted for the still formidable, but scaleable cliffs below the site of the present lighthouse. Another explanation for building a lighthouse at Yaquina Head is that the Head was originally named Cape Foulweather on older nautical charts and the tower was built in the wrong place.

The Yaquina Head Lighthouse was constructed in 1873. This was just four years after the Yaquina Bay lighthouse was constructed a few miles away, south of Newport. The beacon of the new lighthouse was so powerful that the older, less powerful lighthouse beacon on the bay was shut down (see *Ghosts, Critters & Sacred Places of Washington and Oregon for the haunting there.*) The Yaquina Head Lighthouse was recently opened to tourists, thanks to the efforts of Bureau of Land Management employee, Michael Novack, and others. Because it was isolated from tourist visits, stories of its two ghosts have not circulated until recently.

The first ghost story originated while the lighthouse was being constructed. It was built with an inner and outer wall, and the space in-between was filled with rubble. This building technique allows the tower to bend with the hundred mile an hour winds that can hit it and rebound without cracking or breaking. When the inner and outer walls were finished, the workers began filling the narrow space between with a mix of dirt and broken rocks. Suddenly, one of the workmen accidentally fell in with the rubble.

There was no way to get the man out, so his co-workers were forced to finish filling in the space, entombing their friend within the lighthouse. Some people believe that the man was not killed instantly, and he survived long enough to realize what was happening. These people also believe that the lost worker still hammers on the rock inner walls of the lighthouse in an effort to free himself. This haunting may be explained away as the normal creaking of the huge tower as it relieves stress from the wind and weather.

The second ghost is harder to explain as structural settling. In the 1930s, Henry Higgins was the third assistant lighthouse keeper. One night, the head lighthouse keeper left the lighthouse to go Newport. The second assistant who was left behind took the opportunity to get drunk. It fell to Henry to look after the beacon that night. Sometime after dark, the head lighthouse keeper went outside to look at the lighthouse. He saw that the beacon was out. He rushed to the lighthouse, where he found the number two man, passed out. He rushed to the lighthouse spiral staircase to find Henry and get the beacon working again. He found Henry's body on one of the stair landings, dead of a heart attack.

The surviving assistant lighthouse keeper was kept on and was more attentive to his duties. Except for one thing. He would never go up the stairs without his pet bulldog or another person. He believed that Henry's ghost haunts the stairs. Was this a case of guilty conscience or a true haunting? Does Henry's ghost still desperately try to climb up the stairs to light the beacon and fulfill his sacred trust?

Several years later, lighthouse keepers swore that they have heard the sounds of someone walking up the eighty-foot high spiral stairs when they have stood watch over the beacon. When they looked down, there was no one there. Since the lighthouse was opened to the public, many people have felt something strange on the stairs or heard disembodied footsteps. When I went to the lighthouse myself, I asked the interpreter if he had seen or heard anything strange. He just smiled a denial.

Poulsbo, Washington

A family affair (A small farm near the main entrance to the Bangor Naval Base, Washington)

Jay and his friend were looking for a place to live. He found that his friend John and his girlfriend lived in a small farmhouse a few miles outside of Poulsbo. They needed someone to share the rent. When Jay visited, he told John's girlfriend that he thought the place was great, except for the fact that it was haunted. It turned out that Jay's feeling was correct.

After a few weeks, the ghost began pestering John's girlfriend, Sharon, when she was alone in the house. One afternoon she was doing laundry in the basement. She had left the basement door open to allow sunlight from the kitchen down into the basement. She paused while doing laundry because she heard the sound of footsteps walking down the stairs. Between the sunlight from the open door and the light bulbs in the basement, the basement was well lit. Sharon heard the footsteps, but could not see anyone. She dropped her laundry and ran out of the basement.

After a year or two, John's other friend left. Jay, John and Sharon took in another roommate, named Ken. Ken brought a little history with him. His grandparents had built the farm decades before. Ken's grandfather had died a few years earlier, though his grandmother was still alive, in a nursing home. Ken had laughed when he heard the ghost stories. He figured that his grandfather was still around and just playing tricks on Sharon. It was like having another roommate who did not take up too much space.

One weekend morning, Jay slept in late. When he woke up, he found himself alone in the house. He verified this when walked to the bathroom upstairs and looked out over the empty driveway. He heard the sound of footsteps, slowly climbing the stairs to the second floor. They continued down the hallway toward the bathroom. Jay could hear the familiar pattern of squeaks and creaks the stairs made under everyone's feet. They stopped outside of the bathroom door. He watched as the doorknob slowly began to turn. He called out a warning to "Grandpa" that he was using the bathroom.

The doorknob stopped turning as he spoke. It did not return to its original position. It just stopped moving. There were no retreating footsteps. Jay cautiously reached out and turned the doorknob the rest of the way and opened the door. He searched the entire house after that. He did not find anyone hiding anywhere in the house.

Seaview, Washington

Louie's still hosting at the **Lamplighter Inn** (39th and L Street, Seaview, Washington)

The Lamplighter Inn has been a part of the Long Beach community for over 125 years. This has been time enough to accumulate a number of ghosts. The primary candidate for some of the more physical phenomenon is the late Louie Sloan. Louie owned the restaurant/lounge for decades before he sold it in 1963. After that he was a regular fixture in the bar until 1977, when he died at the age of eighty. Strange poltergeist activity began shortly after that.

Shortly after Louie's death, Jenita VanBuskirk closed the lounge for the night. Two people playing pool delayed her closing routine. They ignored her repeated statements that the bar was closing, so she turned off the lights over the pool table. They finally got the message and put down their cues. She walked away from the light switch and was surprised when the lights came back on. She walked back to the switch and found it was still in the off position.

In 1990, Mary Smith was working at the lounge. There was only one patron in the bar that night. He was sitting at the bar. Smith heard a clicking noise and looked at the pool table. She watched as the pool balls began moving across the table, bumping into each other. Their collision had made the noise she heard. This continued for several minutes. Over a five year period, Lamplighter employees and patrons gradually began to accumulate a wealth of stories about strange happenings.

They felt that it was no coincidence that this began shortly after Louie's death. Much of the phenomena ceased or at least slowed down after Louie returned to the Lamplighter, at least part of him did. When he died, Louie was cremated at a funeral home called Penttila's Chapel by the Sea. No one collected his ashes, which were placed in the attic along with those of fifty other people.

In 1992, the owners began looking for friends and family to take some or all of the ashes. The owners of the Lamplighter accepted the urn containing Louie's ashes and placed it in the lounge. Since that time most of the physical manifestations have ceased. Everyone believes that the permanent move has pleased Louie and he has come to rest.

Tillamook, Oregon
Tillamook Rock Lighthouse (In Tillamook Bay, Oregon)

The island where the Tillamook Rock Lighthouse stands has come full circle in spiritual terms. It was a sacred place to Native Americans for hundreds, perhaps thousands of years. According to their legends, the rock was haunted by *Elip Tillicum*, by powerful spirits, who caused accidents or canoe wrecks to anyone who came to the rocky island. This legend seemed to come true when construction began on the lighthouse. The Master Mason hired to oversee construction of the lighthouse was swept off the rock by a wave the day he began work. Today the island and lighthouse are again sacred; they have been converted into a *necropylon*, a giant monument where cremated human remains are kept.

Between the isolation it enjoyed in prehistoric times and its present solitude, Tillamook Rock had an intense and important human occupation. Construction on the lighthouse began in 1879, and took nearly a year and a half to complete. It was dedicated in January of 1881, and continued operations until September of 1957. A small crew of lightkeepers led a lonely existence there. The Rock was only accessible by boat a few days a year. The boat or ship with supplies and personnel would frequently have to anchor just off of the island and wait for the weather to clear before they could off load their supplies. When the weather did clear, they used a derrick to lift the supplies from the deck and winch them up to the base of the lighthouse. The derrick was destroyed by a storm in 1934.

It was imperative to keep the beacon lighted each night, which was a difficult assignment for the keepers. Ocean storms could toss debris up to the top of the lighthouse tower, destroying windows and damaging the light itself. Sometimes the ocean waves would flood the lower levels of the lighthouse, nearly drowning the keepers. One of the lightkeepers who has kept stories of the supernatural and other history of the lighthouse alive is James Gibbs.

Gibbs was stationed at Tillamook Head and other northwest lighthouses (see the *Cleft of the Rock Lighthouse* in Yachats, Oregon). He chronicled his experiences in several books, including *Tillamook Light*. His experiences at Tillamook Rock included the sounds of ghostly moaning and the sight of a phantom or derelict steamship that brushed the Rock, loosing its rudder. Gibbs and his fellow lightkeepers spotted the rudder later and tried to recover it without success.

The Lighthouse was shut down at midnight on the 1st of September 1957, and sat vacant for decades until Mimi Morisette bought it in 1981, to turn it into her *Eternity At Sea* necropylon. Several years ago, work crews traveled out to the Rock and gutted the interior of the lighthouse, leaving only the spiral staircase leading to the top of the tower. They sealed and cemented all the windows and other openings and installed shelving units to store cremated human remains. The work crews still go out to the island when they can, to repair any storm damage to the structure, as well as ferry ashes to their final resting place.

Between the time when the lighthouse was vacated and its conversion into a tomb, the lighthouse received a few visitors, like John Buckingham. In 1980, John contacted the owner of the Tillamook Rock and received permission to visit the old lighthouse. He charted a twenty three foot boat from Seaside and quickly reached the island, only to face the real peril of jumping from the boat onto the rock without being washed away by waves. After a few practice half-jumps, he leaped out of the boat and safely clambered onto the Rock. While he avoided large piles of seagull droppings, John walked to the open lighthouse. He found the lighthouse keepers had left the furniture behind. It was warped, while the paint was peeling off the walls of the lighthouse and all exposed metal was turning into rusty scraps.

After looking at the ground floor of the lighthouse, John walked up the spiral staircase toward the lantern room at the top of the lighthouse. In the semi-darkness, he expected to hear the moaning ghost that haunts the tower to make itself known. He reached the second floor landing, when he heard the sound of a human voice, moaning in pain. John was the only person on the island; there was nowhere for anyone to hide. He did not wait to investigate the sound but hurried down the stairs and out of the lighthouse. He slammed the door shut behind him. He signaled to the waiting boat and leaped aboard as soon as it came close to shore. He was perhaps the last person to hear the ghost.

I have tried contacting the Eternity at Sea people for an interview but at this time they have not responded to my messages.

Yachats Oregon
The Haceta Head Lighthouse (92072 Highway 101 south, Yachats, Oregon)

The Haceta Head lighthouse is thought to be several "mosts" of all of the lighthouses on the Northwest Coast. At a cost of $180,000, it was the most expensive lighthouse constructed. Its 2.5 million candlepower beacon is the most powerful on the coast, and it is the most photographed lighthouse in Oregon. Most people feel it is also the most beautiful lighthouse on the coast. It is also the most haunted lighthouse on the Oregon Coast.

Almost all books on haunted lighthouses, and more especially books on Pacific Northwest ghosts, discuss the hauntings at the Haceta Head lighthouse. As with many ghost stories, the details of the haunting at Haceta Head grow with the telling. As time goes by, more paranormal events are recorded. Because of this, I waited until this book to discuss the Haceta Head lighthouse, so that I could take the time to gather new stories in addition to a brief summary of the many older stories about the old structure.

The lighthouse and lightkeeper's quarters at Haceta Head were constructed in 1893, and the lighthouse is still in operation today. Stories about the lighthouse began to circulate in the 1970s, when the surviving keeper's quarters were leased to Lane Community College as an extension campus. The keeper's quarters building is in reality divided into two self-contained living quarters. At the same time as classes began, the U.S. Forest Service, who owned the buildings implemented plans to restore the buildings to their original condition.

In 1976, Jim Alexander, his son Dave and another man were hired to begin repairs. As soon as they began work tools began to disappear, only to reappear in strange places. Jim wanted to make sure that his son and co-worker were not playing tricks on him. Sometime earlier a dirty paintbrush had disappeared, only to reappear later, completely cleaned. While Jim and his co-workers were eating lunch together, Jim kept watch on the brush, which he had placed in open sight. He turned away once, looked back and saw the brush had disappeared. No one had left the spot where they had been sitting.

Jim was cleaning the outside of some newly installed windows a few days later. Each time he sprayed cleaner on the windows, someone inside the building would walk by. When he wiped the liquid away, he would look inside but there was no one there. Jim went into the attic to repair the last broken window. While he was up there he felt a cold wind blowing from behind him. He turned around and saw the apparition of an old woman floating about a foot above the ground. Her hair and old fashioned dress were pressed against her by the wind and her arms were stretched out toward him. Jim turned around and bolted down the attic trapdoor and left the lighthouse, never to return again. The ghost visited him in his dreams for the next four nights. Each time she asked his help in repairing the house.

A desire to keep the house in good repair seems to be the primary purpose of this ghost. The same evening that she appeared to Jim, the caretakers, Jim and Anne Tammen, heard the sound of a broom sweeping glass in the attic above them. The next morning they found the glass from the broken window swept into a neat pile in the center of the attic. The Tammens lived at Haceta Head for 16 years, until they left in 1989. In that time they too had paranormal experiences.

They often saw the ghost of an elderly lady doing household chores, as she had done in life. This ghost was called Rue; no one seems to know why. She may be the spirit of Mrs. Frank DeRoy, the wife of one of the first lightkeepers. Mrs. DeRoy was supposed to have been a domineering person who kept an immaculate house. There is another story about the ghost. There is a small grave behind the lightkeeper's quarters. Legend says that it is the grave of a child who died shortly after being born. The female ghost may be that of the mother, still searching for her lost child.

A few years ago, the lease by Lane Community College ended and the U.S. Forest Service allowed the use of the building to change. Mike and Carol Korgan took up a lease on the property and now operate it as a Bed and Breakfast. The Korgan's shut down their successful Portland bakery to live a life of ease as hosts to visitors and the ghosts.

The lighthouse has three bedrooms and is booked-up about six months in advance. Many guests who stay there come for the ghostly experience. There is a diary in the Mariner's Room where guests are encouraged to recount their experiences. Sometimes these guests expect to stay in a dark and Spartan house. They are usually surprised at the clean airy rooms as well as the seven-course breakfast the Korgans serve.

I spoke with the Korgan's daughter Michelle, who

operated the house from 1999 to late 2000. She recounted some of the incidents that have happened since her parents moved to Haceta Head. When they moved, they brought along a large Queen Anne couch. They have given it away several times, but it always seems to come back. The couch is over eight feet long and very heavy. Many people they have given it to have not taken it, after trying to load it in their pick-up. A few people have taken it home with them, only to return it a few days later.

For some reason, it just does not fit the house. Mike and Carol believe that is haunted by the spirit of it's original owner. Michelle does not believe this, since the original owner committed suicide because his house was about to be seized for back taxes, and he could not bear to leave it. After all this time, why leave the house for the furniture? They all agree there is something odd about the couch.

Since the Korgans took over at the Haceta Head, there have been many incidents recorded by guests. Most couples who visit follow a typical pattern, where the wife usually drags her reluctant husband to the coast. Many of the women want some kind of spirit contact, while the men are openly skeptical when they arrive. By breakfast time, it is usually the husband who admits to being converted. Perhaps Rue is lonely for male companionship? Sometimes she may be less than friendly though.

Around Christmas time in 1998, a husband and wife were staying at the Lighthouse. The husband was standing by the house Christmas tree, looking out the window. He was surprised when his wife screamed a warning to him about the tree falling over. The man turned and jumped out of the way, narrowly avoiding being hit. He and the Korgans examined the tree. It was about eight feet tall and had been securely inserted into a very heavy cast iron stand. The tree was not top heavy, nor was it overly decorated. They could not figure out how it had tipped over. Even though it was not life threatening, the man was shaken by the incident.

Michelle told me that things have been pretty quiet for the last five months or so. This may or may not be due to a natural event around Christmas of 1999. There was a landslide in December of 1999 that cut the electricity to many parts of the Oregon Coast, including the Haceta Lighthouse. She remembers sitting by the fireplace, soaking in a sense of peace that filled the house. Could Rue have been gathering energy from the electricity, only to fade away when they had a power outage? Or is she just resting?

Guests are still reporting small incidents over breakfast. Some have smelled the scent of flowers or rose perfume. Others have entered their rooms, only to see an imprint on their beds, as if someone had been laying there only seconds before. There is also the log book, full of other people's experiences. Like the couple who watched their daughter's glasses pushed up and over her forehead by unseen hands...

Cleft of the Rock Lighthouse and Museum (Yachats, Oregon)

This functioning, non-government lighthouse is managed by Jim Gibbs, a retired government lighthouse keeper and author. Jim spent several years working on many of the Northwest's facilities. He wrote several books about his experiences, including the beautiful and forbidding Tillamook Rock Lighthouse. Although Jim is noncommittal on the subject of ghosts at Tillamook he has had some strange experiences in his lighthouse museum.

The land itself may be haunted. There is a legend about a child who died several years ago and was buried on the land behind the lighthouse. One visitor stood outside the lighthouse and became so entranced with the pattern of light beacon, that she became hypnotized. Although no one has died in this relatively new building, some of aura of past tragedies may linger on some of the old equipment that are now exhibits. On several occasions, Jim and other people have watched a ship's wheel begin to spin around on its own, as if moved by invisible hands plotting a change in course.

Sources Consulted

Books

Norman Michael and Beth Scott
>1995   *Historic Haunted America*. Tom Doherty Associates Book, Tor books, New York, NY.

Gibbs, James A. Jr.
>1953   *Tillamook Light*, Binfords & Mort, Portland, OR.
>1955   Sentinels of the Northern Pacific, Binfords & Mort, Portland, OR.

Holland, F. Ross Jr.
>1994   Great American Lighthouses, John Wiley and Sons, New York.

Periodicals

Bacon, Larry
>18 September 1989   "Couple leaving history at Heceta," *Register-Guard*, Eugene, OR

Baker, Dean
>29 October 1978 "Lady of the attic," *Register-Guard*, Eugene, OR.

Mitchell, Jann
>31 March 1998   "To the lighthouse," *Oregonian*, Portland, OR.

Mortenson, Eric
>31 October 1994 "Lady ghost keeps watch at Heceta," *Register-Guard*, Eugene, OR.

Moore, Sherri
>31 October 1993, "Tales from the Crypt," the *Tri-City Herald*, Kennewick, WA.

Unknown
>7 November 1994   "Caretakers share home with ghost," *Statesman Journal*, Salem OR.

Internet Sources

Too Close for Comfort *www.rpi.net.au/~ghostgum/castle.html*
Lighthouses of Oregon: *www.cr.nps.gov/maritime/light/capearag.htm*

The Columbia River Gorge

Cape Horn

Jane and her husband, Mark, are a typical Middle American husband and wife. They have a house in Vancouver with a mortgage, two cars and 2.5 children. Okay, they have three children.

Although they love each other, the pressures of life can lead to conflicts ranging from quiet disagreements to heated arguments. When their disagreements turn into arguments, they are careful not to let their children become involved. Instead of fighting in their children's presence, they get in their car and drive as they talk it out. Sometimes the drive becomes very, very long.

In January of 2000, Jane and Mark could not agree on some family issues. They left their neighborhood, and Jane, who was driving, headed to Washington State Highway 14. Once they were east of Camas, traffic thinned out quickly. Many people choose to drive the twisty turns of Highway 14 for the solitude. They can count on passing only a handful of cars or the occasional logging truck between Camas and Stevenson. Most commuters prefer to drive through the Columbia River Gorge on Interstate Highway 84 in Oregon, because it is safer and quicker. Over the years many people have gone off the road, and been injured or killed, particularly on the open bridge that hugs the rock face at Cape Horn.

Once they reached Highway 14, Jane and Mark stopped arguing. They both watched the road when the car slowed down as the road grade began rising. Jane paid especial attention to the road as she made the series of turns to follow the curve of the road. They drove around the final bend of the road, onto the bridge that marks the passage around Cape Horn. Mark also watched the road, paying more attention to the ride, rather than the argument. They crossed the bridge and the highway curved right. Jane turned the steering wheel to follow the road. Mark was beginning to relax when Jane suddenly slammed on the brakes.

They had been going nearly forty miles an hour, when Jane suddenly stepped on the brakes. The tires squealed and the brakes locked as the car skidded to a stop. At that point on the highway there is only a guardrail and a few trees that separated them from a drop of several hundred feet to the floor of the gorge. The car skidded to a stop a long second or so later. Mark could not keep his voice down. He yelled, "What are you doing?"

Jane had kept her eyes on the road the entire time. She turned to Mark and replied in surprise, "What do you mean? Didn't you see him?"

When they rounded the curve, Jane had watched in surprise as a man stepped out from behind the trees and stood in the center of the road. She stepped on the brakes in an effort to stop before they hit the man. When the brakes locked, she was horrified when they continued on, hitting the man. Or almost hitting the man. The instant that the car touched the man, he disappeared. There was no bump or thump like a body would have made if they had driven over him; the man had simply disappeared.

Their original argument was forgotten when they

discussed the near-death experience. Although Jane had seen a man with dark hair and a beard, wearing coveralls, Mark had seen nothing. The day had been rainy earlier, but the sky had cleared shortly before they began their drive. All Mark had seen was a clear stretch of road and nothing else. Was it a hallucination, or something else? Maybe it was related to some past trauma or accident on the highway, or was it related to the nearby *Mount Pleasant Grange*?

The Mount Pleasant Grange (Marble Road and Washington State Highway 14)

Sometimes the story of a haunting is not the historical background or events that lead to the formation of a ghost. Sometimes it is the events or experiences of the people who perceive the ghost that really make the story. Pat has been sensitive to the supernatural since he was a child. Many children seem to have the gift of seeing ghosts and spirits but it usually fades over time. This is not true in Pat's case. Even at the age of thirty nine, he sees and feels things that most other people do not.

In August of 1999, Pat and his wife took a drive through the Columbia River Gorge to look at the stars. On the way home they decided to finally stop and look at the Mount Pleasant Grange and its historical marker at the edge of the highway. It is hard to tell how many times they and other people drive by signs like this and are curious, but do not have the time to stop and read them.

When they headed into the driveway, Pat began experience the familiar fuzzy feeling he gets when going into a haunted location. Pat's wife is not sensitive to the paranormal, but she became quiet too. This was a clue that this was not just another simple haunting or latent memory.

Pat became aware of more than one spirit surrounding them. He sensed many spirits of all ages, both male and female. They were located both inside and outside of the building. Whatever caused their presence was not good. Pat has been in several haunted houses in the past, and it never bothered him after he came to grips with his ability. This was different. He described the aura surrounding the grange hall as thick, clingy and awful! Pat can usually separate out a residual aura of past events from an active haunting with self aware spirits. He is sure that this is not just past memories lingering behind, but there are active spirits remaining around the grange hall. It only took a few seconds before he and his wife *had* to leave.

What could be at the old Grange hall to cause this feeling? To most people today, the Grange is an organization that provides cheap insurance to a mostly rural, group of people. The Grange was much more in the past, when most of America was filled with small family farms, in the mid 19th century.

In December of 1867, Oliver Hudson Kelly and six other men founded a secret society they called the National Grange of the Patrons of Husbandry. The name "Grange" came from the French word for barn. It is a secret society, because its members identify each other by a series of passwords and rituals. Members of the Grange were called Grangers. Each local chapter of Grangers constructed a local Grange hall, usually on donated land, built by volunteer labor.

The Grange originally limited their membership to people interested in, or practicing agriculture. By 1873, there were twenty one state Granges, with more than a thousand local Granges in each state. By 1875, there were over 1,000,000 Grangers in the United States. This was about three percent of America's population at that time.

The Grange did everything from financing business loans to forming cooperative buying clubs, (like Costco) to lobbying for political reform. In the 1880s Congress passed a series of federal "Granger" laws. These laws regulated water rights, railroads and grain storage, where they related to farming. Individual Grange halls, like the Mount Pleasant Grange, were often the only public building where farming communities could gather to do everything, from celebrating a great harvest, to planning how to cope with a drought. It was the heart of the community.

More old ghost stories from the E d g e f i e l d P o o r h o u s e (2 1 2 6 S W H a l s e y , T r o u t d a l e , Oregon)
I wrote about the many hauntings at the Edgefield Poorhouse in my last book, *Ghosts, Critters and Sacred Places of Washington and Oregon*. In the year since I finished that book, there have been some changes at the Edgefield. The McMenamins company, which owns the Edgefield, has expanded their facilities there. They refurbished the third floor of the Poorhouse and opened it to guests. In April of 2000 I took a tour of the Edgefield with one of their tour guides, Ashley, who added to the lore of the Edgefield.

The Study was the first new haunted room we stopped at. In the past the men and women were kept separate most of the time. They ate and slept on different floors to keep them from committing any indecent acts. The Study was the private dining room the women inmates used when the Edgefield was first opened. After several years, the dining room was made co-ed and the Study converted to other uses. The women inmates complained about this change, because it meant that they had to dress-up for breakfast, instead of eating in bathrobes and curlers. Today the room has been converted into a comfortable meeting room, with chairs, couches and a small library. It is open to groups on request.

In 1999, one of the maintenance workers decided to take a break after work. He let himself into the Study for a quick nap before driving home. He was asleep by 9 P.M., but awakened a few minutes later. He was sleeping deeply on one of the couches when he was awakened by a distinct "PSSSSST!" He sat up in the dark, listening. The sound was repeated. It sounded like a human whispering, trying to get his attention. He reached out in the darkness and turned on one of the lights. There was no one there. He searched the Study, which was empty. Maybe he was snoring and disturbed one of the older inmates?

The Third Floor was not normally used by residents in the past. It was left more or less unfinished when the Poorhouse was built and used for storage and short-term housing. Workers and guests have already reported numerous strange and possibly paranormal, events on the third floor. The strangest happened early, when the building was first being renovated over a decade ago.

First there was **the Cat in the attic**. When the McMenamins first purchased the old Poorhouse they had to have the roof repaired. When the maintenance workers opened the attic door on the third floor near Room 307, a suitcase fell down and nearly hit them. They opened the dusty, warped bag and found a mummified cat inside it. For several years, the cat was on display in one of the many pubs that dot the Edgefield. Then one year the mummified body got a little wet, and maggots began to infest it. Nauseated workers disposed of the strange mascot. A painting of a cat on the attic door commemorates the story.

In April of 2000, A guest staying in **Room 307** heard a cat meowing outside her room late one night. She had to get up to use the bathroom at the end of the hallway and was surprised to hear the noise coming from the bathroom. She thought that one of the many cats that patrol the Edgefield grounds was trapped there.

She cautiously opened the door and peeked inside. The meowing stopped when she opened the door. It was empty. She was amazed. There was no way the cat could have gotten out without her seeing it. Is this the same cat that spent years locked up in an old suitcase? Or something else?

The **hallway near the trapdoor** seems to be haunted as well. During renovation on the third floor, workers had to finish their tasks before evening, to keep noise down for the guests. Ashley's boyfriend worked at the Edgefield and was part of the work crew. One of his duties was to get "QUIET" signs out of a locked storeroom and put them up throughout the building. One night he went upstairs to get out the signs, when he found them already placed around the halls. He was the last worker there in the building, and he had been upstairs an hour or so before, after the other workers had left. They signs were not posted then. They had been locked in a storeroom and he was the only one who had a key. He does not know how this could have happened.

The **hallway leading to Rooms 311-315** is avoided by some of the Edgefield staff. This hallway is at a right angle to the main third floor hallway. There are no windows in this hallway to let light it, so it is dark and gloomy. A set of heavy double doors divides this short hallway. One night in April of 2000, one of the staff was walking through these doors when they suddenly and forcefully closed on her. There was no draft, and the doors are normally secured to stay open. It was a strange coincidence, if that is what it was. Strange things continue to happen in the hallway.

In 1999, a staffer went to the third floor to look at the renovation. She was surprised to find that one of the painters had already been at work. There was a picture of an elderly

man, painted on one of the dark paneled walls, inside these double doors. She did not like it. It was perhaps too lifelike. The eyes seemed to follow her. Despite the weird feeling, she thought it was well done, and went to get a friend to show her the new artwork. When they returned, the painting was gone.

At the end of this short hallway there is a black painted door. The door is set a couple of feet above the floor level and needs a set of temporary stairs to reach it. The door leads to the attic spaces and electrical system and is always kept locked. One night, a housekeeper walked down the hallway with an armful of towels and saw that the door was open. She put the towels in the room, but did not go inside. It was too spooky for her. The only person with the key to the door had left sometime earlier; no one else working that night had a key. She investigated the next morning, and the door was closed and locked again.

Rooms 305 and 306 were originally one large room called the Women's Hostel. One night in 1999, a night security guard was patrolling the third floor when he heard a rhythmic squeaking noise. He followed the sound down the hall. He had a list of which rooms were occupied, and was surprised when he tracked the sound to the Women's Hostel room. He was surprised because the room was vacant that night. He opened the door with a passkey and let himself in. He was shocked by the sight that confronted him. In the corner of the room was an old rocking chair, rocking on its own. There was no one in the chair or anywhere in the room. The sound had been going on for a few minutes before he opened the door. It could not have been a case of someone getting out of the chair, which continued rocking for a few seconds under its own inertia. It did not show any signs of slowing down.

Employees at the Edgefield are told to expect the unexpected, but this was too much. He watched it for a few seconds before he hurriedly closed the door. Shortly after this incident, the room was divided in two and remodeled. My guide, Ashley, did not know where the old rocking chair went. But I am sure it is still floating around the Edgefield somewhere.

The Althea Room is located on the top floor of the old Administrator's Residence. Among the most notable p a r a n o r m a l happenings in the Althea Room is the ghost of a young girl. She has awakened guests in the middle of the night by grabbing people's feet. She sometimes serenades guests by singing nursery rhymes to them. A few guests have also seen her.

On January 16th of 2000, my wife and I arranged to stay in the Althea Room. I arrived with a tape recorder, a camera loaded with infrared film, and my 8 mm video camera. I took several pictures in the Althea room and set up my camcorder in one corner of the room. I left the camcorder on for several hours, both when we were in the room and while we were out. When it came time to develop the infrared film, I saw that I took some very nice, spooky looking photographs, but nothing paranormal showed up.

The remote video footage was much the same. Fortunately for me, I left on a two week military mission on the morning of the 17th, so my wife happily watched several hours of video of our empty room.

There was one incident that was certainly very strange. While we were the only guests on the top floor of the Administrator's Building, we were not the only guests in the building that night. Two people staying on the second floor. The house has been divided into several separate bedrooms, with common bathrooms on the first and second floors.

The guests in the Althea Room have to go downstairs to the second floor and use the bathroom, next to the stairs. On the morning of the 16th, we woke up early to have breakfast in time to leave and catch my airplane flight. At 6:30 A.M., I tiptoed down the stairs and used the shower. I tried to be quiet, because the other guests' room was on the other side of the stairwell from the bathroom.

After showering, I dried off and began to dress. At that time I heard the sound of someone walking down the from the Althea Room to the second floor. I could hear the footsteps clearly, since the stairs were right next to the bathroom. The steps paused at the foot of the stairs. I hurried out of the bathroom to the door that separates the stairs from the second floor hallway. Moisture had caused it to swell and stick badly. I thought that the steps were my wife coming down to shower and I wanted to help her open the door. It took a few seconds, but by using leverage, I opened the door quietly so as to not awaken the other guests. The stairway was empty; there was no one there.

Could the other guests have caused the noise? I looked at their door, which was not wood, but textured glass. There was no light or sound coming from their room. I paused and listened. The house was quiet. I walked up the stairs to the Althea room. My wife was still in bed. I told her of the little mystery but she was still sleepy and not interested at the time.

Jefferson Davis

I still wonder about the steps. Was it an echo from the outside? Had the other tenants snuck out, with no more noise than their footsteps climbing down the stairs? I still wonder.

Sources Consulted
Books
Keyser, James
> 1992   *Indian Rock Art of the Columbia Plateau*, University of Washington Press, Seattle.

Ramsen, Jerold
> 1972   *Coyote Was Going There, Indian Literature of the Oregon Territory*, University of Washington Press, Seattle.

Internet resources
Horsethief Lake State Park, *www.parks.wa.gov/horsthef.html*

The Inland Empire of Eastern Washington

Spokane
Ghost Buster Busted? (Spokane, Washington)

In the last few years, I have met many people who have engaged in parapsychological investigations, otherwise known as ghost busting. I have been fortunate that I have not met any that I considered to be crooked or frauds. In my opinion, some of the people I have met are very intuitive. Others have been…a little low on psychic talent but they have all been sincere. Most of the people who act as paranormal or psychic investigators do not do this as a full-time job. Quite sensibly they have jobs that pay for their bills, which finance their passion for the paranormal. There are a few cases where people try to support themselves at it, like Susan Johnson of Spokane.

In 1997, Johnson became Spokane's first licensed and bonded psychic. She offered to lift a Gypsy curse put on the city by the disgruntled Romany a few years before. This curse was made in retaliation for the city confiscating large amounts of cash and valuables in a sting operation. Johnson offered to lift the curse for a modest $7,500 fee. This may have been the largest commission Johnson tried to get. She needed it. It turns out that Johnson had mortgaged her house to raise money to start her business.

In 1997, a California-based mortgage company, who accepted her historic Underhill Park home as collateral, loaned Johnson $44,000. Three local banks had turned Johnson down for loans earlier. It must have seemed like a supernatural event to Johnson when loan offers arrived from California. Bank officers told her that they were sure of her business, and they believed that she would be able to pay off the loan in three years, even though the interest rate was 11%. They failed to ask why she received a modest income from Social Security. They did not know or possibly care that she received benefits for a mental disorder.

After two years of very slow business, Johnson was unable to make her loan payments. The bank offered her house at auction, where it was purchased by one of their subsidiary firms for $36,000. This was just about what Johnson owed on her mortgage. The Northwest Justice Project is currently trying to have the loan dissolved and title to her house returned to Johnson.

If it were not for the tragedy of Ms. Johnson losing her house, this situation reminds me of the recent bankruptcy of a famous phone-in psychic hotline that had to hang up it's phones permanently due to; unforeseen financial difficulties.

The Ghost Restaurant? (unspecified location in Spokane, Washington)

In 1986, Cliff and his wife were staying in Spokane for a few days. Rather than impose on friends, they decided to look for an inexpensive restaurant for breakfast. As they drove through Spokane, they saw a restaurant with a yellowed, hand painted sign advertising "Steak & Eggs" for $3.85. They decided to stop and see. They entered and found that it had a typical "greasy spoon" atmosphere, but was filled with customers. The menus said *Chuck Wagon*. They sat down and ordered the special.

When it came time to pay the bill, they noticed that it was made out for the wrong amount. Instead of charging $7.70, the bill was less than a dollar. They told the waitress, who checked with the manager. She returned and informed Cliff that the charge was still for the lower amount, because she had made a mistake. They paid and left. When Cliff told his friends about the restaurant, they told him that there was no restaurant named *Chuck Wagon*, in Spokane. Cliff took them to the location of the restaurant and sure enough, there was no restaurant there. A different business stood in the same location. Was this a slip in time and space? Or just a case of mistaken road directions?

This story is based on an account in USA Today's collected work, I Never Believed in Ghosts Until...

The Spokane Civic Theater (Spokane, Washington

From the outside, the Spokane Civic Theater is a pretty unremarkable building or rather set of buildings. It looks like a series of wooden blocks of various sizes, stacked together. This makes sense, since was built in phases, from the mid-1960s, until the present day.

Like all theaters, the true magic is not on the outside, but on the inside. This is very true in the case of the Civic Theater. There has been a Spokane Civic Theater since the late 1940s. It has become one of the most successful community theaters in the United States, with a yearly attendance of 35,000 guests and 1,800 subscribers.

A community theater is not a building, it is a group of people who gather together to put on plays; whatever building or open space they use is just the stage. Drama and the theater are almost paranormal, since they grew up out of ancient religious festivals. Many theaters seem to be haunted, perhaps energized by the theatrical energy. The Civic Theater had many homes, until the present building was constructed. Prior to this, the Civic Theater was the old Riverside Theater. Some people have suggested that George, the resident ghost at the Civic Theater, traveled across Spokane to the present building when it opened in 1967.

No one knows who George was in life, or how he

came to become a ghost. Was he left behind from the building that used to stand on the same site as the present theater? Or did he indeed move in, when a handful of dust from the stage of the old theater was sprinkled on the stage of the new one to christen it? Wherever George came from, he is a proper theater's ghost.

Sometimes a floodlight will sweep across an empty and dark stage, even when the lighting book is empty and the electricity is supposedly turned off. Many of the staff and actors have felt a presence in the backstage area during productions. Many theaters ghosts appear on the stage, or make themselves known when a successful play begins its run. George does not do this; instead he flushes the toilets in the men's bathroom when no one is there. I am not sure what this signals.

South Hill Mansion (2526 East 17th, Spokane, Washington)

Everyone loves a celebrity, or if they don't love one, they are fascinated with them. Most celebrities are rich, or famous for their sports skills, or political power. One requirement necessary to become a celebrity is that you have to do something interesting or unique. Even the rich and famous have celebrities, some of whom provide a service to them, like a hairdresser. One Spokane celebrity was Dr. Rudolph Hahn.

In the 1920s and 1930s, members of Spokane's rich, elite and famous used to come to Hahn's ornate mansion to enjoy his splendid (and outrageous) parties. Why was Hahn so famous and his company sought after? He provided discreet abortions to Spokane's rich and famous.

Hahn arrived in Spokane in 1899, and immediately set up practice as a physician, despite the fact that he had no medical license or credentials. The thirty five year old Hahn was actually a former barber. He promoted many faddish medical therapies, including electroshock therapy. Hahn was famous for his hobbies, like car and boat racing. The charismatic Hahn attracted a wealthy clientele, who suffered more from boredom than illness. He dispensed quack medicines and occasionally performed abortions for them.

His business paid well. In 1924, Hahn purchased South Hill Mansion from wealthy Spokane druggist William Whitlock. Hahn continued his practice at the mansion, to ensure the privacy of his clients. Hahn's fame was not enough to protect him from police raids. During renovations in later years, an owner found a secret panel concealing a compartment big enough for at least one person to hide in.

Hahn was fifty-nine years old at the time he moved in with his second wife, twenty-seven year old Sylvia. It may have been their stormy relationship as much as Hahn's business that led to the strange stories and possibly hauntings within the mansion.

In the 1920s, a drunk Hahn drove his racecar into the swimming pool he built when he purchased the house. He had the pool filled in so it wouldn't happen again. Sometimes Hahn would appear in public in an expensive suit, wearing bedroom slippers.

In 1933, Sylvia divorced Hahn, after he chased her through the house with a sword. They remarried in June of 1933, after their long distance phone calls became too expensive. Their relationship became more violent. In August they were both jailed for public drunkenness and mutual battery. Sylvia broke several of his ribs in that fight. In March of 1934, sixty-nine year old Rudolph filed for divorce. He claimed that he was afraid of thirty-seven year old Sylvia. They reconciled a few days later.

In May of 1940, the police found Sylvia's body in her bedroom. She had been shot in the head. They also found that the door lock had been shot off, and the bedroom walls were riddled with bullet holes. At a coroner's inquest, Hahn admitted that he had threatened Sylvia with a gun. He claimed that the bullet holes were the from past target practice. Based on the testimony of a witness, who claimed Sylvia had talked about committing suicide in the past, the coroner ruled her death a suicide. After the inquest Hahn continued with his business, but not without more scandal.

In 1929, he was acquitted of a charge of performing an abortion on a seventeen-year-old girl. Despite this brush with the law, he continued practicing his services for the rich, until one client died. In 1945, he was charged with manslaughter, when she died after a botched abortion. Although this charge was dropped, he was found guilty of two counts of performing illegal abortions. Instead of being put in prison, the eighty year old Hahn was fined $1000 and put on probation.

After his conviction, Hahn finally became too famous. His business was destroyed and he was forced to sell his mansion. He tried to drop out of sight, but could not. In August of 1946, the police found Hahn's body lying on the floor of his apartment. A man named Delbert Visger had stabbed him through the heart with a bayonet during a robbery. Even before his death, rumors had already begun to circulate about Hahn's hidden wealth and the strange goings on at his house. His death only fueled these rumors.

Neighborhood children used to play in the abandoned gardens that surrounded the house. In the decades after Hahn's death, they became overgrown (and scary) woods. The children dared each other to run up and touch the walls of the house. They talked about ghosts haunting the old building.

Simple stories? Later owners tried to downplay

stories about the house. Despite this, former caretakers who lived there during renovations in the 1990s claimed to have witnessed many unexplained phenomena. It began with strange noises that could not be explained as the house settling. Then there were the shadows they both saw, the ones that used to move across the walls. Like an invisible person walking across the room. A former owner admitted that he had seen a phantom woman at the top of the mansion's staircase.

Some hauntings become more active during a remodel, only to quiet down or even disappear after the remodel is finished. I wonder what happened at the South Hill Mansion? I probably will not find out, since the Mansion is a private residence and I would discourage any readers from visiting there as part of a ghost hunt.

Tri-Cities (Pasco, Kennewick and Richland)

The refrigerator ghost (private residence near the corner of 57th and Hood Street, Kennewick, Washington)

In the summer of 1998, Lilith and her family found a pleasant, gold-painted house on Hood Street. When she and her husband were shown the house, they fell in love with it. They told the realtor they would take it immediately. They should have brought their children and pets over for a look first. From the first, neither their pets nor their children liked the house.

The dogs were affected the most. Sometimes they would bark and rush through the house, from the front to the backdoor in the kitchen. They would stop at the door, looking at it, barking. At first, Lilith or her husband would yell at the dogs to quiet them. Then they opened the door to see if anyone was there. The back porch was always empty. When they closed the door, within a few seconds they would hear a knock at the door. When they opened the door again, the porch was still empty. In addition to the back door, the dogs acted strangely on the stairs.

The dogs would either cringe or bark at something neither Lilith nor her husband could see. The children saw strange things on the stairs. They described it to their parents. It was not a full, three dimensional solid figure, it was more of a cloudy outline. The whole family agreed that the house was haunted. This calm acceptance may sound strange, but they had lived in haunted houses before. They decided to let whatever events were going on continue until they came to some kind of conclusion. Being practical people, they also began looking for a new house to rent.

The incident that stuck in Lilith's mind happened in the kitchen one morning. The whole family was in the kitchen when the refrigerator door opened all the way, on it's own. She and her husband stopped and stared at it. Their daughter piped up, "don't worry mommy, the ghost will close it." A second or two later, the door slowly swung shut. A few days later they found a new house and moved out of the haunted one.

The Railroad Ghost (near the Yellepit siding, west of Pasco, Washington)

When I first heard this story I spent hours looking at maps of Eastern Washington for Yelepit, Yellepit and even Yellow-Pit. I finally found it. Yellepit is not a place, so much as a location. It is a railroad siding and disused station standing near railroad marker 215. This is about sixteen miles east of McNary Dam. Trains do not stop there anymore, though they do slow down when they are heading east, because the railroad grade increases there.

Amtrak train engineers have reported seeing a woman sitting on top of a pile of rocks to the right of the train, where the grade begins rising. Several of them have had a good look at her, when their train slowed down as it struggled up the tracks. She is always wearing a long dress, which is strange because she is only seen during rainy weather in the fall and winter. She has not been seen by all of the engineers, just the ones whose train is running late (this is a smaller number than many might think), into the evening, when the weather is just getting dark. Some engineers who have seen her report that she looked a little strange and out of place. Others claim that she was transparent.

In 1999, after several months of waiting, one engineer, Peter, saw her. His observations of her behavior were similar to other people who have seen her. As he drove the engine past the woman on the rocks, she did not react or turn to look at the train. She stared into space. It was as if the train did not exist. Because he had been expecting to see her for some time, he observed several details about her.

He noted that she was wearing a high necked, light colored print dress with some kind of dark spotted design. Her skin was dark and her hair was light colored. It seemed to Peter that she was bathed with some kind of light. I asked him if her image could have been some kind of a negative, where dark colors had been turned light and light colors were now dark. He was not sure, but said there was something strange about the light.

According to the lore passed down by the railroad employees, in the 19th century there was a steamship accident on the river nearby. The ship may have gone aground on a small island in the middle of the river, near the Yellepit railroad landing. The passengers were forced to swim to shore. Among them was a family consisting of a man, his wife and their small child. The man made it to shore first but could not find his family among the survivors. He went back in the water and rescued them. The river level has risen quite a bit since the construction of McNary Dam. The climb up, was more difficult in the past than it is today.

When he reached the railroad tracks with his family,

the man left his wife and child on the rock outcrop. Blind and deaf with fatigue he staggered down the railroad tracks in search of help. He did not see an approaching train. Several of the other survivors stood on the rocks by the railroad tracks yelling and waving their arms to warn him and stop the approaching train, to no avail. The man was struck and killed by the locomotive. Ever since then his wife sits by the tracks and watches the same tragedy time and again whenever a train approaches Yellepit.

I tried looking at this from a skeptical viewpoint. It is possible, but not likely that this is a case of mistaken identity. Is there someone who just likes to sit on the rocks by the railroad tracks, in the autumn rain? This does not seem too likely. This place is not readily accessible by road. Since the siding is not used anymore, the road has become overgrown. The railroad grade is some distance down a steep slope from the where the road ends. Aside from the train tracks, the only way to reach this spot is from the river. Is there a hiker or boater resting on the rocks? Why does she do it in the worst weather? I can think of more pleasant ways to enjoy nature.

So if you happen to be riding Amtrak east to the Tri-cities and the train slows down, look for the Yellepit sign and continue looking out of the right hand side of the train, you may just see her, waiting... and watching.

Farmhouse ghost (farmhouse outside Walla Walla, Washington)

Many people have hobbies that other people consider odd. Although amateur photography is not odd, some people specialize in odd subjects. Eve's father specialized in pictures of old barns. Some of Eve's earliest childhood memories consist of driving down the highways of eastern Washington and stopping because her father saw a barn or farmhouse he just had to take a picture of.

One day when Eve was five years old, her family was

driving from Walla Walla to Pullman. Her father stopped when he saw another prime barn. The barn and farmhouse turned out to be deserted. By the looks of the buildings, they had been empty for more than a decade. While her father was setting up his camera and tripod, Eve and her sister Valerie decided to explore the abandoned farmhouse. At first, it was not too exciting.

The girls entered the house through an unlocked front door. For a while they stood on the threshold looking around. They did not go inside. Their father had warned them not to walk around inside old buildings. The floor could have given way under them. This was a two-story house, and the stairway was directly across the living room from where the girls were standing. Eve does not remember whether she appeared, or walked out from a second story room, but both girls looked up the stairs and saw an old woman standing at the top of the stairs. The woman looked down at them without expression.

The woman was unremarkable, except for the fact that she was wearing a nightgown. Without warning she began to glide down the stairs, or rather she began to float downward, without touching the stairs. Without saying a word, the woman opened her arms and continued floating toward the girls. Strangely enough, the girls were not frightened. Maybe they were frozen in place? The next memory Eve has, is being in the car, driving down the road. Again, strangely, this whole sequence of memories was buried in both Eve's and Valerie's memories for years.

Neither girl spoke or consciously remembered this experience for nine or ten years, until Eve was fifteen years old. On Halloween of 1989, both girls attended separated costume parties. The teenagers at the parties began to trade stories of the paranormal. It was like a light bulb turning on in Eve's memory. She shared her story with her friends. Later that evening, her sister called her. She had remembered the same story. They compared notes, and their remembrances seemed to be nearly identical. When I spoke to Eve about the barn and farmhouse, she told me that she was going to contact her father for a copy of the picture of the barn. She wants to see if the farmhouse is still there. I look forward to hearing what she finds.

Sources Consulted

Books

Clark, Douglas
   1998   "For sale: Spooky South Hill mansion," *Doug Clark's Loose Clark Journals*, New Media Ventures, Inc. Spokane, WA.

USA Today
   1992   *I Never Believed in Ghosts Until...*, USA Weekend, INC, Chicago.

Periodicals

Clark, Doug
   27 April 1997   "Bonded, licensed psychic friend can lift city curse," *Spokesman Review*, p. B1 Spokane, WA.

Eshelman, Dave
   30 October 1975 "Kennewick man chases ghosts from houses," *Tri-City Herald*, Kennewick, WA.

Kershner, Jim
   22 Sep. 1996   "Solid gold, Spokane Civic Theater approaches its 50th year," *Spokesman Review*, p. E1, Spokane, WA.

Sowa, Tom
   12 May 1999   "Bank forecloses on `sorceress' lawyers accuse lender of `equity stripping'," *Spokesman Review,* p.A1.

Strange Critters

A Radioactive Heron? (Tri-Cities, Washington)

In the mid-1990s, many residents of the Tri-Cities and people passing through the Hanford Government Reservation were surprised to see a large pinkish red bird in the Hanford Hills. Many people thought that the bird, which was four or five feet in length was some kind of a heron. Except for the coloring. Herons are bluish-black, while this bird was rosy-white, with scarlet feathers on its shoulders. People began calling or visiting the offices of the Hanford Reservation, asking if the bird was a heron suffering from radiation poisoning.

Local wildlife biologists began looking for the bird and eventually found it. They identified it as a pink flamingo (*Phoenicopterus ruber*). The mistaken identification on the part of the local people was understandable, since flamingos were once included in the heron family by biologists. Having solved the identification problem, the biologists were posed with another problem. How did the flamingo arrive in Washington State? Fossilized flamingo remains have been found in Oregon. Of course, this was about 12,000 years ago. Today pink flamingos live on the Atlantic and Gulf coasts in sub tropical and tropical America.

Maybe it was visiting its ancestral home? The bird was sighted several times over the summer, while the weather was still warm. It disappeared in early fall when the weather began to turn cold at night. Perhaps it was gaining strength in preparation for a long flight home.

A Rain of Salamanders (Boring, Oregon)

In June of 1911, a young girl was walking along the banks of the Sandy River when it began to rain. This is not an unusual occurrence in the Columbia River Gorge. What *was* unusual were the critters mixed with the rain. In addition to raindrops, the girl was pelted with several heavy objects. She looked around, and saw hundreds of salamanders falling from the sky. They covered the ground around her. Most of them were alive, and began to scurry around, seeking shelter.

What caused the rain of amphibians? How did the flamingo arrive in eastern Washington? There have been incidents in the past, where there have been rains of things, such as fish, frogs, stones, alligators, grain, nuts, leaves, straw, stones, money, raw meat and even blood. These incidents have been recorded all over the world for over two thousand years. There have been several theories to explain these incidents. Charles Forte made a career of recording and reporting strange incidents, such as these mysterious rains. He suggested (facetiously) that there were floating continents in the sky. When there was a storm on the floating continent, it dumped garbage on the solid earth below. There are of course more serious theories.

One theory, is that storms like a tornado on land or a water spout at sea can pick up solid matter, as well as water. They can hold this matter suspended for several hours. The storm could travel hundreds of miles before dropping the matter as it dissipates. A circular storm like a tornado would operate like a centrifuge as it spun around in a circle. This would separate objects of different specific gravity and gather together objects of similar density.

For example, if a tornado touched down on a pond it may have gathered thousands of gallons of water, and everything within the water. As the storm spun around, the algae or plants would have been gathered together and separated from things like the frogs, etc.

As the storm lost energy, objects would have gradually been dropped off into the atmosphere. Heavier objects would have fallen first, then lighter objects, all based on their weight and specific gravity. This would account for the concentration of the same kind of objects in the strange rain. There have been cases when people were pelted with already threshed grain, while their neighbors were covered with nothing but chaff, the outer grain coating. It could also account for the strange condition of some of these rains.

Sometimes the animals, particularly fish, are frozen. As I mentioned earlier, sometimes there are rains of blood or raw meat. If a storm picked up living creatures like fish, and went up to high altitudes, the cold could have frozen or preserved the fish. In addition to being cold, the air pressure is very low at high altitudes. If a large animal was picked up by a storm, from deep under water, and transported quickly to a high altitude, it may have suffered from explosive decompression. In other words, in travelling from underwater to a near vacuum, the pressure of it's own internal organs may have caused the animal to explode.

Were the salamanders in 1911 or the flamingo in the 1990s picked up by a storm and transported hundreds of miles through the air to land in a strange place? The unfortunate thing about these kind of incidents is that the victims cannot tell us where they came from.

Sasquatch

Most Bigfoot sightings last only a few seconds. A confused mind could easily interpret the rush of a large bear or an elk or a horse running by the flash of a car's headlights as a Sasquatch. There are also cases where people have duped others into promoting the legend of Bigfoot by deliberately faking footprints and sightings. On the other hand, I must point out that this does not explain away all of the sightings as coming from confused witnesses or fakes. Just as in the case of paranormal phenomena like ghosts, Ockham's Razor cuts both ways. Can there have been thousands of stories about the Sasquatch for hundreds of years without there being some truth to the matter? The real question is, how much truth?

The last year has been fairly quiet, as far as the activities of Sasquatch are concerned. Bigfoot Central is an organization headed by Cliff Crook, in Bothell, Washington. Like other Sasquatch friendly organizations, Bigfoot Central tries to track and investigate Bigfoot sightings around the world and the Pacific Northwest. Their database contains many sightings reported in 1999, with fewer in 2000.

The Olympic National Forest has been a central area for the hairy man of the forest in 1999. On May 26,[th] a man fishing along Feeder Creek, inside the Forest came face to face with a Sasquatch. He described this particular specimen as being over seven feet tall, with shaggy black hair, and dark black facial hair. The fisherman described the Sasquatch's gaze as piercing. The next day, another forest visitor spotted large, human-like footprints in the forest. Were these from the same critter, or a different one? Despite the shock, the man has returned to Feeder Creek for the fishing. He brings a friend or gun, or both with him now.

On the 28th of September, Forest visitors sighted a furry walking upright on two legs. When it spotted them, it ran away. When they investigated, they found tracks in the mud along a stream. These tracks were six inches wide and thirteen inches long. They are much too big to have been bear prints.

There were three Bigfoot sightings near Orting, Washington, in the vicinity of Mount Ranier in 1999. In one case, on the 26th of September, two bow hunters confronted a Bigfoot... from a safe distance of about 300 yards. Which was close enough for them. They watched it through binoculars for several minutes. The critter stood facing them, standing upright on the edge of a rock outcrop on a cliff face. It was covered with shiny black fur, with a simian like body, wide shoulders and a broad chest. They described its face as being apelike. When it left, they investigated the place where it had been standing but did not find any footprints or other signs. If they had been watching this critter with only their naked eyes, I believe that it could have been a bear. Since they used binoculars, the bear explanation is unlikely.

Peeping Sasquatch?

January is a cold month east of the Cascade Mountains, as anyone who has spent the winter there can tell you. January of 2000 was no exception. "John" lived in a house just outside of Walla Walla, near the Snake River. His house was heated by a wood stove, which needed refueling at odd hours. On the morning of the 24th he went out to stock up on wood at 3:30 AM. For the last few nights prior to the 24th, he had heard many of the neighborhood dogs barking at night but he was not worried about prowlers or dangerous animals.

It was a short walk from his front porch to the woodpile under a fir tree. He began gathering an armful of wood, when he turned and faced the house. He saw someone, or something, standing beside the house looking through the dining room window. Although the figure was large and man-like John could tell it was not a man. Dropping his wood, John ran into the house and slammed the front door.

He made sure all of his doors and windows were locked and waited until daylight. After sunrise he walked down to Highway 260 and called the National UFO Reporting Center. He appeared on Art Bell's radio show on the 25th of January with Peter Davenoport of the National UFO Reporting Center and Matthew Moneymaker of the Bigfoot Researcher's Organization.

The Patterson film controversy continues

In addition to the sightings I have mentioned, there

has been no resolution to the recent controversy surrounding the Patterson Bigfoot Film. In 1967, Roger Patterson filmed a short movie of what he claimed was a Sasquatch in a California forest clear-cut. This film has become the most important evidence for the existence of Bigfoot, and so critics and controversy also surround it. In 1996 and 1997, a reporter for *Strange Magazine*, Mark Chorvinsky investigated reports that Hollywood special effects costumer John Chambers constructed the costume.

Chambers had worked on the movie *Planet of the Apes* in 1967, as well as the television show *Lost in Space*, designing and constructing ape and monster costumes. After several months of research, talking with many special effects experts and Chambers via fax, Chorvinsky was unable to reach any positive conclusions.

He believes that the Bigfoot in the film is a fake. This is based upon the opinions of every special effects expert he spoke with. At the same time, he was unable to find any person willing to swear that they had firsthand knowledge that Chambers made the costume. Chambers himself denied that he designed the suit. Chorvinsky pointed out that many special effects experts are secretive about the work they do, and Chambers has been involved in other Bigfoot fake stunts. Despite this, opinion is not the same as positive proof.

In 1998 the validity of the film came under fire from other sources. A Canadian researcher examined the film frame by frame under high resolution, using the digital photo software. He found what he identified as a zipper in two of the frames. At the same time, a man from Eastern Washington claimed that he was the man wearing the suit. The magazine *The Skeptical Inquirer*, suggested that it is difficult or impossible to tell how big the creature in the film really is. This was based on their analysis of the film focus, camera angles and relationship of the creature to objects in the fore and background.

Patterson Film defenders have challenged the findings of the digital photo analysis. They point out that the movie being analyzed is not a copy of the original, but is a copy of a copy, or even a third generation copy. Movies, just like pages on a photocopier, will fuzz and loose detail each time they are copied. They also point out that the original movie instructions from Kodak recommend that the maximum size that the film should be enlarged is only 100 times and the buckle shows up at a 400 X magnification. They consulted software experts from *Adobe* and *Pegasus*, who suggest that when a photograph is blown up that much, the digitizing process can create false images.

The identity of the man from Washington claiming to have worn the suit has still not been released. His lawyer stated that he would only go public after a movie contract was signed. Even Patterson skeptics find this wait to be suspicious. The waiting and controversy go on.

Cadborosaurus

French scientist Bernard Heuvelmans coined the word Cryptozoology, (meaning the study of lost or hidden animals) to define the biological search and study of animals that people thought were extinct. As time goes by, people are exploring more remote locations. Animals that were once thought to be extinct have been found. Cryptozoology is not a mainstream scientific discipline, but people who study it try to maintain a scientific approach. Not all of these animals have been found in remote locales. Critters like the Cadborosaurus.

The Cadborosaurus is a sea animal that has been seen many times along the Northwest Coast. It made several appearances Cadboro Bay, British Columbia, which led to this name. The Manhousat people who lived on western Vancouver Island had tales of a creature called the *Hiyitl'iik*. The *Hiyitl'iik* was a sea serpent that was at home in the water as well as on land. It was seven to eight feet long, and could grow wings and fly if it wanted to.

Two prospectors made the first Cadborosaurus sighting in the historic record in January of 1897. Osmond Fergusson and his partner, Walker, were in a boat on the Queen Charlotte Islands when they saw what they thought was a large piece of driftwood. They were surprised when they realized that the log was moving toward them under its own power. When it was about 150 feet away, the "log" uncoiled a long neck and raised a snake-like head out of the water. After looking at the miners and their boat, the creature dove underwater. As it submerged, the startled men estimated that is was at least 25 feet long and had a fish-like tail.

In September of 1905, Philip Welch and a friend were fishing in the Johnstone Strait, near northern Vancouver Island, when they had a run-in with "Caddy". It was around 9 A.M. when they decided to return to shore. They saw a long neck and giraffe-like head rise out of the water about 200 yards from their boat. The creature's neck was about 6 feet long and about 20 inches in diameter where it came out of the water, tapering to 10 inches thick at its head. The critter's head had two rounded, 5 inch bumps on the top of its head. It was hard to see the creature's eyes, maybe because they were the same brown as its hide, but two nostrils were visible. They two men began rowing feverishly for shore. They watched the strange critter approach to within a hundred yards, then it suddenly submerged and disappeared.

There is a long list of sightings along the coast. In the 1930s, a 20 foot long animal with a curved neck and horse-like head was seen at Neah Bay. In 1933, two government historians from Canada saw an 80 foot long sea creature off the coast of British Columbia. In 1934, near South Pender, a sea critter swallowed a duck that had been shot by hunters. Several local people saw the critter a few days later. In 1937, several people in Yachats, Oregon, spotted a sea creature they estimated was over 50 feet long. In 1939, two men in British Columbia saw an adult and baby Caddy playing in the water. One of the creatures made a cow-like bellow.

In March of 1953, two women and their children from Klamath Falls were vacationing on the Puget Sound when they sighted a Caddy. One of them was a trained biologist and gave a detailed description of the sea critter. They were on a hill overlooking the straight of Juan de Fuca near Port Townsend. They saw what looked like a tree limb about a quarter mile offshore. It submerged, only to reappear again a few minutes later, even closer. They saw the exposed portions of an animal that was over ten feet long. There were 3 humps of a partially submerged body and a long, curved neck. The neck was about 6 feet long, and its head was about 2 feet long. The animal was a dark brown color, with orange reticulations in a giraffe like pattern. The creature's head was flat, and behind it was either a lowered fin or mane on the neck. The sighting lasted about 8 minutes before it submerged and disappeared.

There have been many other sightings of Caddy over the decades. In some cases it is described as having fur, other times it has a smooth coat. Its color has varied from green to brown, but the physical proportions are remarkably similar. The only thing missing is a living, or dead critter.

From time to time marine carcasses have washed up on Northwest shores. In November of 1934, a 35 foot long, serpent-like shape washed ashore at Henry Island, in British Columbia. It was serpent shaped and was thirty-five feet long. In 1936 a 12 foot long critter with a goat-like head washed ashore at Aberdeen, Washington. In 1947 portions of a 40 foot long skeleton were collected from a beach near

Vernon Bay and put on display in Alberni British Columbia. Attempts were made to study supposed Caddy remains.

In 1937, whalers near Queen Charlotte Island found the partially digested remains of a strange creature in the stomach of a whale they were butchering. It was about 10 feet long, with a camel-like head and serpent like shape. A sample was sent to a lab, who determined that it was a normal sea animal, deformed by the whale's stomach acids. The same is true of many of the carcasses that wash up on the shores.

When an animal dies and rots at sea, more than their flesh falls off. Most fish bodies are a mix of true bone and cartilage. If a fish body rots for long, the cartilage falls of, leaving only the bone. This can leave a skeleton that does not look like the original animal. There have been a few other cases of live Caddys being caught, if only for a little while.

Captain William Hagelund and his family claim to have captured a young Caddy while yachting off the coast of Decourcey Island, in British Columbia. One night, Hagelund was attracted to the sound of something splashing in the water near his boat. He saw a small creature, about 16 inches long, covered with what turned out to be yellowish fur. It had an elongated snout, forward flippers and a bilobate tail, swimming around his yacht. Taking to a dinghy, Hagelund captured it. He planned on taking it to the Fisheries Department at Nanaimo, British Columbia for study. After listening to the critter's cries for several hours, he decided to let the young Caddy go. He saw it later, in the same waters as it grew older.

In 1991, Phyllis Harsh found a stranded baby "dinosaur" in the San Juan Islands. The animal had become beached, and she used a tree branch to push it back into the sea.

Students and faculty at the University of British

Columbia have formed the British Columbia Scientific Cryptozoology Club to help gather information about sightings of Cryptozoologic animals from across the world. They accept members' applications from the public as well as academics. A visit to their web site at *http://www.ultranet. ca/bcscc/* can put you in touch with them.

Sources Consulted

Books

Benton, William (publisher)
    1994   *Encyclopaedia Britannica, (F for Flamingo),* Encyclopaedia Britannica Inc., New York.
Clark, Jerome
    1999   *Unexplained!,* Visible Ink Press, A division of Gale Research, Farmington Hills, MI.
Davenport, Marge
    1988   Afloat and Awash in the Old Northwest, Paddlewheel Press, Tigard, OR.

Periodicals

Caims, Peter
    September 24, 1967   "Colossal Claude and The Sea Monsters," *The Oregonian*
Mark Chorvinsky, Mark,
    "The Makeup Man and the Monster: John Chambers and the Patterson Bigfoot Suit," Strange Magazine 17, Summer, 1996.
LeBlond, Paul
    1993   "Sea serpents of the Pacific Northwest," Montana Magazine, Autumn p.44-51.

Internet Resources

Bigfoot *http://www.moneymaker.org/BFRR/*
Bigfoot Central *http://www.angelfire.com/biz/bigfootcentral/*
Bigfoot *http://greenfield.fortunecity.com/bypass/48/*
Bigfoot: *http://www.UFOcenter.com*
Cryptozoology *http://www.ultranet.ca/bcscc/*
Cadborosaurus *http://www.seanet.com/~daveco/caddysite.htm*
http://www.seanet.com/~daveco/caddysite.htm original source
British Columbia Scientific Cryptozoology Club, *http://www.ultranet.ca/ bcscchtm*

Jefferson Davis

Some Thoughts on Ghost Hunting
Ghost Photographs

This is the longest and most in depth discussion on the technical aspects of ghost hunting in any of my books. One is that for the first time in nearly five years of visiting haunted locations; I have taken a photograph that shows something that I could not explain as a normal phenomenon. The second is that I have watched a growing number of people taken in by phony or flawed ghost photographs. This is especially true on the Internet where it is easy to post photographs. Many of these "ghost" photographs can be explained as something as simple as light reflection or a finger in front of the camera.

What is a ghost photograph? The immediate response to that question is "a photograph with a picture of a ghost in it." Unfortunately, this answer does not work too well. People are still debating the nature of ghosts, and it is difficult to define a ghost photograph without defining the nature of a ghost.

More practically, a ghost photograph is a picture taken of a place or person, where something that does not belong, (anomalous), shows up on the print and negative. When that happens, the photographer must eliminate all logical or natural explanations for this anomaly. When that is done, by the process of elimination, most ghost hunters can proudly say, "I've got a ghost photograph!"

To do this, you should know something about the nature of light, black and white, color and infrared film work. This will help you troubleshoot your photographs if you have taken what you believe are ghost photographs. This is like the difference between being able to drive a car, and being able to repair one if it breaks down. I know that the following section will be too technical for some casual readers. It will also probably be too vague for the physics minded people as well. Sometimes there is no middle ground. At the end of this section I will list many common errors that can create false ghosts.

Light and Human Vision

In the past, if you asked some physicists, they would say that light moves in waves. Later, if you talked to other physicists, they would say that light moves in particles. After decades of debate over bland faculty lunches, the physicists finally agreed upon a unified theory of quantum physics. This theory states that light consists of both waves and particles. They also agreed on some fundamental properties of light.

We know that light is a small part of the entire spectrum of electromagnetic energy (see the illustration on the next page). Light falls between other forms of energy such as x-rays, radar waves, microwaves and radio waves. Light is a form of energy that is detectable to the human eye. Light is also measurable with regards to the length of its emissions, whether waves or particles. Visible light is only a small portion of the entire electromagnetic spectrum.

The human eye detects light energy ranging from $7 \times 10_{-5}$ to $4 \times 10_{-5}$ centimeters (or cm) in length. This is also expressed as 0.0000400 - 0.0000700 cm. All of these powers and zeros are confusing; so most people use the term nanometer or nm. One nanometer = 0.0000001 centimeters. Which means the human eye detects light from around 400 to 700 nm. (I included all of these numbers to impress the physicists in the audience with my ability to quote useless facts.) We do not see tiny little waves or particles of energy; we see this energy as colors.

At one end of the visible spectrum we see the color violet, at 400 nm (nanometers). At the other end of the visible spectrum we see red, at 700 nm. All of the other colors we see are the energy wavelengths in-between. When

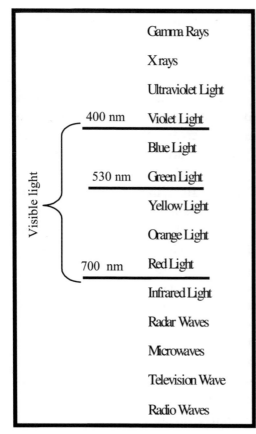

you look at a rainbow, what you are seeing is moisture in the atmosphere acting like a prism. It splits all of the mixed light striking the earth into its separate wavelengths.

Photography and Film

The oldest ghost photographs were taken with black and white film. I think that it is still the most popular film used for taking ghost photographs. Here is how it works. When light bounces off an object, whether solid, gaseous or liquid, it passes through the lens of the camera and strikes the film inside the camera. Black and white film is made of several layers of material.

The base layer is made of cellulose acetate (this is the thick, *filmy* stuff). A dark *anti-halo* layer is applied over the base. The anti-halo layer prevents any reflections from bouncing through the base layer and reflecting back into the light sensitive layer, which coats the surface of the film. This light sensitive coating is the part of the film that produces the actual negative image used to make photographs. This coating is a mix of about 40% silver bromide and a small percentage of other light sensitive chemicals, bound into a gelatin base.

The crystals are microscopic in size, and help determine the film sensitivity. The larger the crystals, the higher the film speed. Smaller crystals are less sensitive to light, but they also produce finer detailed photographs. This is why professional photographers generally use lower speed film for their work. The grains are smaller, and produce a sharper image.

When light strikes the film, the energy in the light energizes the crystal and activates it. When the exposed film is placed in a chemical *developer* bath, the activated crystals turn into a black, metallic silver. The silver bromide that was not activated by light is dissolved off of the film base in a different chemical bath. This produces the negative image on the film, where light areas in the negative become dark on the photograph, and vice versa. When light is shone through the negative, onto a light sensitive paper, a positive image photograph is produced.

Color photography uses multiple layers of chemicals that are sensitive to three kinds of light: red, blue and green. Each layer produces a negative image of the sensitive color and positive image in a complementary color. The blue layer produces a positive yellow, green uses a positive in magenta and red uses cyan. With new advances in color film and developing, it is now cheaper to use color film rather than black and white. This may be why color photography is beginning to replace black and white photography in ghost hunting.

Infrared Ghost Photography

I cannot completely discuss the argument of whether ghosts photographs are taken because a ghost passes in front of the camera too quickly to be detected by the human eye, but slow enough for a camera to capture it's image. I must point out that if people find a ghost on a photograph, taken using a slow film like 50 ASA, a human eye would have been able to detect the ghost better than the film. I can talk about spirits being captured on film sensitive to energy in wavelengths outside of human vision, though.

In addition to our eyes being able to detect electromagnetic radiation, our bodies are sensitive to other forms of radiation. Our skin, is a sensory organ, and can detect infrared radiation that is not detectable to our eyes. We know this as heat. This hits upon part of the argument surrounding ghost photographs.

Many people believe that ghosts are a form of electromagnetic energy, and photographs can show ghosts because the photographic film is more sensitive to this energy than the human eye. An example of this is infrared film.

To be brutally honest, people who believe that normal photographic film is more sensitive to infrared or ultraviolet radiation than the human eye, are wrong. The sensitivity of any film to radiation is based on the chemical composition of the light sensitive layer placed on the film. With very few exceptions, normal commercial films are designed to record images **only** within (or under) the range of human vision.

I have heard that some people put a red filter or even red cellophane over the lens of a camera loaded with normal black and white film to take ghost photographs. They believe this converts the films' sensitivity into the infrared range. This is not true. If you do this, you will get some interesting visual contrasts, but if the film is not sensitive to infrared radiation, it will not show infrared images. Since most ghosts are perceived as by many people as hot or cold spots, only a true infrared film could detect them.

There are several brands of infrared film. I am familiar with two black and white films that are sensitive to infrared radiation. One is a specialty film: Kodak High Speed Infrared film. The other is a commercial black and white film: Ilford's SFX 200. The Ilford film is an exception to the rule about infrared sensitive, commercial film.

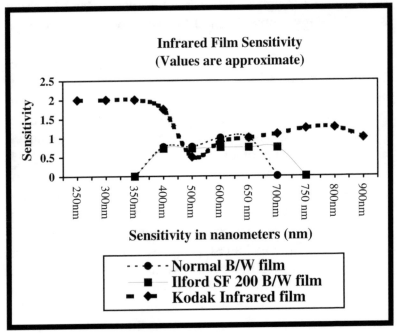

As can be seen from the graph above, most commercial film is sensitive to light from around 370 nm to 650 nm. This is **under** the range of normal human light perception. That makes it less sensitive to light than the human eye. The Ilford film is more sensitive than commercial B/W film to red and infrared, ending just above of the human visual range, at 740 nm. This is just a little bit more sensitive than the human eye.

As you can see from this graph, the Kodak film can detect light energy beyond human vision in both the ultraviolet and infrared ranges. It is sensitive to ultraviolet light beginning around 250 nm and ranges up to the infrared energy range at 900 nm.

Taking Pictures Using Infrared Film

In order to use both of these films to detect infrared

radiation, you must use a special colored light filter. A Kodak Wratten, number 25 light red, filter will gather red light and concentrate it when you take a picture. At the same time, this filter will also allow visible light through, to be absorbed by the film and turned into a picture. This means that a picture taken with the number 25 filter includes both visual and infrared light. A true infrared photograph, where only infrared light is recorded on the film, must be taken using a very dark red filter.

Kodak recommends their dark red filters, Wratten numbers 87, 87c or 89b to do that. For an amateur ghost hunter, the reality of economics enters into the equation. A number 25 filter costs around $15, while the dark red filters cost around $100. As an alternative, the Hoya R72 dark red filter costs around $40. I cannot personally recommend any of these dark red filters, since I have not used any of these filters at this time.

What would I recommend for would-be ghost photographers? There are pros and cons to both films. The Ilford film is cheaper than the Kodak film. It does not require special handling. You can load it, unload and process it as a normal black and white film, even if you use a red lens. On the other hand, although the Ilford film is more sensitive to infrared than commercial black and white films, it is much less sensitive than the Kodak infrared film.

The Kodak film is undoubtedly the best choice as far as its sensitivity to infrared radiation. There are several drawbacks in handling and using it. You must keep it refrigerated prior to use and develop it quickly after you use it. It must be loaded and unloaded in absolute darkness. It must also be processed in absolute darkness. It is more expensive than the Ilford film and developing costs are higher as well. Many people do their own developing of this film rather than trust it to a photo lab. A home darkroom can become expensive and messy.

Even though Kodak touts their film as a "high speed", it is very slow when compared to the Ilford SFX 200, which has an ASA speed of 200. When using the Kodak infrared film in daylight, with a number 25 filter, it has an ASA speed of 50. You must expose at least one f-stop below what your light meter shows as optimal, to account for the presence of the filter. This means that if you use this film you need to either take pictures while in strong light, or be prepared to take pictures with long exposure times. The mechanics of focusing properly add to the problems with both films.

Because the human eye cannot see into the infrared light range, we cannot focus a camera properly when using infrared film. This may explain the blurry nature of some infrared pictures that you see on the Internet. Most older camera lenses have an infrared focusing mark. If you have an older lens, look at it and you will find the major focusing mark, this is usually a prominent red dot or line. A lens with an infrared focusing mark will have a second red dot or thinner line near the primary focusing mark. On some lenses this will sometimes be marked with an "r".

When you focus the camera, note where the distance marker on the focusing ring of the lens lines up on the focus mark, on the fixed ring. When using an infrared film, focus the camera normally; note the reading of the distance mark on the focusing ring. Put the red filter on and move the distance marker from the main focusing point, to infrared focusing point.

I suggest you focus with the red lens filter off. Because of the enhanced red light, it is nearly impossible to focus a camera with the filter on. You can use a tape measure to find the distance to what you are focusing on. Of course, most ghost photographs are taken with the ghost either in front of or behind the point of focus.

Kodak recommends that infrared pictures are taken with the focus set on the smallest lens opening or aperture possible. This means setting the lens set on minimum f stop, of say f22. This aids by concentrating light on the film and helps the focusing problem. With a low f stop, the lens will have the widest focus for objects in the background and foreground of whatever you have focused on. The drawback is that any picture you take will again need a longer exposure time. You should be prepared to take exposures of longer than one second, which means using a tripod.

The photograph on the below was taken using Kodak infrared film with a number 25 red filter. The photograph shows three wineglasses full of water. The glass on the left contains ice water, the water in the center glass is at room temperature and the water on the right is at the nearly boiling.

 As you can see from the photograph, the water on the left has ice cube in it and is nearly frozen. It looks dramatically different from the other two water samples. The hot water on the right does not look too different from the room temperature water. There is a small bit of steam above the water. There is no distinct vapor trail or distortion in the air above or around the hot water glass. Nor is there any distortion in the air around the glass of cold water. Unless your ghost is very cold, it would be difficult to see it on infrared film when using a light red filter. Would a dark red filter show a difference?

Many people today use the latest brand of point and shoot style programmable cameras. If you are one of these people, I suggest you check the camera instruction book or contact the manufacturer to see whether or not your camera has a program mode that can handle infrared film.

Some of the newer cameras use an infrared light beam, shone on the film to read the film speed and count the number of exposures taken. This could cause blurring or over exposure of your film. If you have one of these nifty pocket zoom cameras, you may not be able to purchase filters for your camera.

If you can, check and see if you can set the film speed manually. You must do this to add the extra f-stops to compensate for the filters. And no, fastening red cellophane paper to the lens of the camera with a rubber band will not replace a real IR sensitive filter.

Mistaken Ghost Photographs

Artificial lighting and reflections can cause most false ghost images. If you are taking a photograph using a flash, look at where you are taking the picture. If there is glassware, windows, mirrors or any reflective surfaces in the picture background, you could have anomalous effects show up on the final photograph. Even if you do not see any, when you use the flash they can show up. That is why I do not use a flash when I take photos in haunted locations. Your alternative is to take long exposure photos using a tripod, or use a high-speed film.

If you are taking pictures through a window, be careful of reflections. Even if you do not use a flash, the window can act like a mirror, reflecting light images into the camera lens, depending on the angle you are shooting from.

Most modern "ghost" photographs are globes of light. One natural cause of globes of light is a lighting effect known as lens flare. If you take a photo in natural light, and point the camera toward the sun, a concentrated beam of light can enter the camera lens and overexpose a portion of the film. If you take a fast exposure photo, of say $1/500^{th}$ of a second, you may notice that this white spot is hexagonal. This is because the light passed through the iris of the lens, which is has an angular shape.

In longer exposures, the lens flare spot may be round, because the camera wavered a bit as you held it when you took the picture. Other things can cause globes of light. A rubber lens hood attached to the end of your lens will reduce lens flare

Some newer cameras have an auto wind/rewind function. While convenient, it can cause globes or spots of light. When the film is rewinding, the motor can reach speeds so fast that it will generate static electricity, which causes sparks within the camera body. When these sparks are given off, they expose the portions of the film that they touch, causing fuzzy globes of light.

Some people have ghost photographs where the entire picture is either black or white. The camera shutter can stick open when taking a picture, which causes overexposure and fogs the picture. If the shutter malfunctions and opens and closes too quickly, this can cause a black or underexposed photograph. In addition to globes, some people have pictures showing circular white lines.

If you change camera lenses and the lens is not completely locked into position, a small amount of light can leak in. This will cause curved or circular lines on the negative. If you are using an old fashioned bellows camera, and there are cracks in the bellows, light can leak in, causing straight lines on the outside of the negative. A finger or camera strap on or in front of the lens can cause dark spots or lines.

For more information on photography and possible accidental ghosts, I recommend going to the library and consulting *The Encyclopedia of Practical Photography*. This 14 volume set of books was published by Kodak several years ago, and is still a valuable resource.

My Own Ghost Photograph?

I took the photograph that I have included in this

section. It is inside the Hurn Farm on Whidbey Island. I was standing in the rear of the farmhouse, with the sun at a right angle to the camera lens. I took the picture through a broken window, looking inside the farmhouse. The two anomalous effects on the picture are located in the lower right hand corner and the lower center portion of the picture. Both are on the negative as well as the photo.

There is a fuzzy discoloration in the left-hand corner

of the photograph. It is translucent, and you can see the floor through it. The original photo is color, and this anomaly is pinkish orange. The second anomaly is whitish and opaque at its center. This is fuzzy, like an outer aura. You cannot see through the whitish spot.

I have spoken with several experienced photographers and labs. It is probably not lens flare, because there is a lack of strong light. It is not a reflection, because there was no glass in the broken window and I did not use a flash. I do not use an auto-rewind, so it is not a spark. Could it be a reflection from another light form, across the camera lens? I do not claim that this is a photograph of a ghost, but I *am* waiting for a reasonable explanation of what could cause it.

To Walk the Fire?

One of the privileges I receive from writing books like this is that I have made a diverse circle of friends and acquaintances. Some of these people practice alternative religions and I am sometimes invited to participate in their rituals. In the spring of 1999, I was invited to participate in a firewalk in Southwest Washington.

Unfortunately, I was not able to attend because of other obligations. It took a little persuading, but eventually my wife volunteered to attend in my place. Such is the life of the wife of a ghost-book writer.

On June 26[th,] my wife Janine and our friend Cindy arrived at a private location in Clark County. The location was in a natural clearing surrounded by mature Douglas fir trees. They arrived around 8 AM, to begin the rituals that take place before a firewalk. They began purifying themselves by burning sage and cedar. Each incense performed a separate function. The sage dispersed bad energy, the cedar brought good energy.

Janine and Cindy were then instructed to stand in a circle with the other participants, turning in a clockwise manner. They raised their arms over their heads and clapped their hands three times. More rituals followed.

Next they were instructed to hold a raisin in their mouths and concentrate on the dried fruit. They had to roll it around in their mouths and sample the texture with their tongues. They waited until the raisin dehydrated, and then bit into it, tasting the intense sweetness. Around that time, Janine was wondering what I had gotten her into, but she continued.

All of the participants had to help build the fire. Each person had to touch each piece of wood to help attune him or her to the future walk. Everyone began walking and dancing around the stacked wood. They beat drums and shook tambourines and rattles to build their energy. Once it was dark, they lit the fire. When the fire was burning, they were given a bit of tobacco, told to make a wish and throw it into the fire. Then they wrote down both a secret fear and good experience on a piece of paper and threw it into the fire.

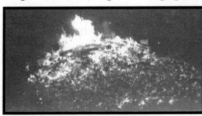

When the fire burned down, they raked the coals into a bed, eight feet across. They gathered in a circle around the coals and again chanted and made music. When each person felt ready, they stood at one end of the coals and walked across as the rest of the participants continued chanting and playing their musical instruments. Of the 28 people present, 25 walked across the coals. Many people walked across more than once over the next two hours, until the coals cooled down. In answer to your question, yes, Janine and Cindy walked the coals.

Janine said that she felt a surging pressure in her chest, and knew that it was her time to walk across the coals. She and Cindy both walked to the edge of the bed of coals and after a second of hesitation and focus, they walked across them. Janine felt the heat, but was detached from any sense of pain. The next morning she had a few red spots on her skin, but that was it. Both of them collected a piece of charcoal from the fire as a memento of the experience.

The rituals that my wife described were an interesting mix. The sage and cedar wood incenses are primarily Native American, but firewalking was not, except among the Cheyenne and a few other tribes. Drums and rattles are nearly universal musical instruments, but Tambourines are not. The ritual of firewalking has been practiced for thousands of years in The Pacific Rim, India, the Near East, Europe and Africa.

It is not commonly known, but in 1519, the Christian Church canonized St. Francis of Paola. St. Francis showed a church committee that he could handle burning branches from a fire and removed red hot metal from a burning kiln with his bare hands. How does this strange phenomenon work? Some people would say that it is belief and the power of mind over matter. Skeptics would counter with an explanation of physics. It has taken thousands of years to try and explain how it works.

Europeans have conducted investigations of firewalking since the 1930s. One researcher discovered the Leidenfrost effect, which he named after himself. Leidenfrost noticed that when small amounts of water are put on a very hot frying pan, the water forms drops, which slide over the surface of the pan. This is caused when heat from the pan evaporates microscopic amounts of water, which carry off heat and form a protective, cool layer of air around the cooler water. He speculated that when a person walks over hot coals, the sweat from their feet forms a cushioning layer of air, which carries off the heat from the coals. Modern researchers have experimented by firewalking with both dry and sweaty feet. They have not noticed any difference in the effect of the coals on the feet of the firewalkers.

Another theory of why people do not get burned by the coals is the result of callouses on feet protecting the firewalkers from the heat of the coals from the fires. Scientists first conducted their research with East Indian Yogis in the 1930s. They noticed that many of the Indians had thick callouses on their feet. The scientists speculated that the thick layer of dead skin protected the softer tissues underneath from being burned. More recent firewalks in the United States has shown that people without callouses have walked fires without being seriously burned. A third theory explaining firewalking seems to be the most reasonable.

This last theory involves the way the hot coals both loose and conduct heat to the firewalkers. Scientists have measured temperatures of the hot coals at a firewalk. They found that in most cases, the coals start out at around 1200 degrees Fahrenheit, and within an hour, they cool down to 500 to 900 degrees. This heat loss is not enough to protect feet if there is a direct transfer of heat from the coals to the feet, since human skin begins charring at 325 degrees. Researchers found that although the coals loose heat by convection, by transmitting it through the air, charcoal does not transmit heat well by direct contact. This is like a lit match, the match gives off more heat an inch or two above the flame, rather than on the head of the match itself.

Scientists believe that this is the key to firewalking. A bed of coals has uneven heat, with hot and cold spots. The coals themselves are broken, with uneven surfaces. When someone walks over coals, especially if they are covered with an insulating layer of ash, the coals will not transmit an even amount of heat to human feet. Scientists as well as the spiritualists conducting firewalks recommend that people walk across the coals quickly. People should walk with fast, even steps, but not run across. If someone runs across the coals, their feet sink into the coals, where the temperature is higher. Coals will stick to their skin, which could cause burns. Standing on the coals for more than a few seconds may cause burns if the coals are still hot.

A researcher in Norway stood on a bed of coals that were 140 to 160 degrees Fahrenheit for about 45 seconds, without getting burned. This is not unusual, since second degree burns do not begin until skin reaches a temperature of 160 degrees. At the same time, this does not explain standing on hotter coals.

After all of this deconstruction, it sounds like firewalking is not dangerous, and we could all do it. This is not true. Walking a bed of coals is dangerous, although perhaps not as dangerous as some people think. There are exceptions to the scientific theorizing.

In October of 1997, the world's hottest firewalk was conducted in Redmond, Washington. The bed of coals was about 13 feet long and the temperature ranged from 1,602 to 1,813 degrees Fahrenheit. The firewalkers used a leaf blower to superheat the coals. Incidentally this blew the dust off of the coals. Twenty three people walked across the coals, where the temperature ranged from around 1,600 to 1,700 degrees. One firewalker stood in the center of the coals, where the temperature was 1,813 degrees. Observers noted later that he had some red patches of skin and a dime sized blister on his inner sole. Other firewalkers have crossed beds of coals over 30 feet in length. Surely this is long enough for human feet to absorb enough heat to burn or blister.

When my wife participated in her firewalk, one of the last people to walk was a woman suffering from muscular dystrophy. She could not walk on her own without help. Two other firewalkers stood on either side of her, supporting the woman as she lurched across the coals. They carried most of her weight for several seconds. They sank deep into the coals, where the temperature was hottest. Some of the coals stuck to their feet, but they were not burned. Had the coals cooled enough so that they were safe, or is there more to firewalking than physics?

Despite the physics involved, it takes an act of faith to walk across hot coals. This is the important thing about firewalking or any other act of faith. The real magic is that despite fear and the threat of injury, people faced their fears and walked across the fiery coals. On the other hand, one thing has demystified firewalking a bit for me. Some corporations are hiring firewalk specialists to conduct firewalks for their executives during teambuilding retreats.

Let me say again, that firewalking is dangerous. I recommend against anyone conducting their own firewalk without an advisor willing and able to assume responsibility for any possible risks, both physical and spiritual!

Sources Consulted

Books

Benton, William (publisher)
    1994   *Encyclopaedia   Britannica,   (C   for   Colour)*, Encyclopaedia Britannica Inc., New York.
Benton, William (publisher)
    1994   *Encyclopaedia Britannica, (E for Eye)*, Encyclopaedia Britannica Inc., New York.
Benton, William (publisher)
    1994   *Encyclopaedia Britannica, (L for Light)*, Encyclopaedia Britannica Inc., New York.
Benton, William (publisher)
    1994   *Encyclopaedia   Britannica,   (O   for   Optics)*, Encyclopaedia Britannica Inc., New York.
Benton, William (publisher)

1994   *Encyclopaedia Britannica, (P for Photography)*, Encyclopaedia Britannica Inc., New York.

Manheim, A.C. (Translator)

1967   *The Way Things Work*, Simon and Schuster Publishers, New York.

Internet Sources

Micheal McDermotts page:*http://members.aol.com/fyrwalking/index.htm*

Ilford Fact Sheet on Ilford SFX 200 Black and White Film, *www.Ilford.com*

Firewalking myth vs. Physics":*http://www.pitt.edu/~dwilley/fire.html*

Kodak High Speed Infrared Film, *www.kodak.com*

How to Fake Pictures of Ghosts, *www3.sympatico.ca/roddy/ghostmain.html*

Parapsychology: *http://www.ispr.net/hauntings/main.cfm*

Parapsychology *http://theshadowlands.net/index2.htm*

Wings of Fire Web Site *http://www.firewalking.org*

Kjernsmo Kjetil:*http://www.skepsis.no/english/subject/firewalk/kpreemp1/*

Index

The following sources were consulted during the writing of this book

Hauk, Dennis William
 1996   *The National Directory of Haunted Places.* Penguin Books Inc., New York.
Helm, Mike
 1983   *Oregon's Ghosts and Monsters.*   Rainy Day Press, Eugene, OR.
Krantz, Grover S.
 1992   *Big Footprints: A Scientific Inquiry into the Reality of Sasquatch.*   Johnson Printing Company, 1180 South 57th Court, Boulder, Colorado 80301.
MacDonald, Margaret Read
 1995   *Ghost Stories from the Pacific Northwest.* August House Publishers, INC., Little Rock Arkansas

Internet Resources
Castle of Spirits: *http://www.castleofspirits.com/*
Ghost Stories from Around the World: *http://www.sitemart. com/ghost/18145.htm.*
Ghosts of North Portland Web site: *http://www.hevanet.com/ herberb/ghosts/mohawk.htm.*
Obiwan's UFO free paranormal page: *http://www.ghosts.org/*
Paranormal Northwest: *http://www.eskimo.com/~pierres/*
Spectre Search: *http://web2.arimail.net/~spectre1.sprportl. html*
The Shadowlands: *http://theshadowlands.net/ghost/*

Books by Jefferson Davis

Ghosts and Strange Critters of Washington and Oregon

Ghost, Critters and Sacred Places of Washington and Oregon

Ghost, Critters and Sacred Places of Washington and Oregon II

Graphics and artwork for this book were provided
by Stone Crow Studio:

"Stone Crow Studio" is a graphics studio dedicated
to producing the finest in computer generated fine art for
integration into your commercial projects. We specialize in
the design of logos and illustrations for books covers, stories,
CD cover art, clip art, and any other special projects you
might need to have designed. We insure our work will be the
finest you can find as we generate our own artwork in the
oldest of traditions and combine it with the technologies of
today. Please feel free to contact us with any questions. .

(360) 694-4387
www.pcez.com/~stonecrow
stoncrow@pcez.com

About the Author

Jeff Davis was born in Vancouver, Washington in 1962. According to family tradition he is related to his namesake, Jefferson Davis, President of the Confederacy. Jeff is an Army brat and grew up playing in and around the Vancouver Barracks. This led to an interest in the military and history. Late night horror movies instilled an interest in ghosts, mythology and archaeology.

After a three year enlistment in the U.S. Army, Jeff earned a Bachelor's degree in Anthropology as well as a commission in the U.S. Army Reserves.

For several years Jeff worked for the U.S. Forest Service as an archaeologist. He worked on several National Forests, including the Gifford Pinchot, the Boise, the Umatilla and Mt. Hood National Forests. In addition to his work as a freelance archaeologist and part-tine volunteer consultant to various Pacific Northwest Indian Tribes

In 1995 Jeff and his wife, Janine, moved to England for a year where he earned his MA in Archaeology from the University of Sheffield. His thesis topic was the lifestyle of the Vikings in Greenland. That is where he received the inspiration for his publishing company name, Norseman Ventures.

Jeff is in the U.S. Army Reserves. His work on a book on Ghosts of the Pacific Northwest was interrupted by a tour in Bosnia in 1997. When he returned in 1998 he began seriously researching and writing books on the paranormal. This is the volume he has completed in the last two years.